Kingdom Community

Dr. Jerry Horner

Kingdom Community

Published by
ICM Leadership Solutions Pte Ltd
81 UBI AVENUE 4, #11-09,
S(408830)

ISBN: 978-981-18-9005-5

TABLE OF CONTENTS

PREFACE

While Jesus was on the earth, the focus of His teaching and ministry from the beginning to the end was on the kingdom of God. At the beginning He quoted Scriptures pertaining to the kingdom and announced that He was the fulfillment of those proclamations (see Mark 1:14-15; Luke 4:17-21). At the end, in the days preceding His ascension into heaven, He taught His disciples, "speaking of the things pertaining to the kingdom of God" (Acts 1:3). The kingdom of God is not a physical kingdom. It is a transformation of heart and mind, a way of believing and living in preparation for eternity. The kingdom of God refers to God's reign on earth and consequently, in our hearts. It is about His kingship and our obedience to His rule. Jesus taught that His kingdom "is not of this world" (see John 18:36), and that it must be entered by repentance and faith.

A kingdom presupposes that there are citizens over whom the king reigns, and that citizenship involves mutual relationships. If you are a believer in Jesus Christ, then your citizenship is no longer "of this world." You are a citizen of the kingdom of God, along with all others who have experienced a new birth in Christ. Much of the New Testament is devoted to teaching fellow citizens how they are to live together as a kingdom community. As God created the world and everything in it, He repeatedly called His creation "good." However, after creating man, He said, "It is not good that man should be alone." Community is not only a foundational part of creation, but also of the new creation. It's our relationship with the King that enables us to relate to each other (1 John 1:3). It's true that we have an individual and intimate relationship with God, but He doesn't just call and work through individuals. He has called us to be in community to support one another and complement each other with the different gifts that He has bestowed upon us.

"If a kingdom is divided against itself, that kingdom cannot stand" (Mark 3:24). Being in community with one another is a challenging situation because of our human weakness and self-centeredness. Misunderstandings, different personalities, and varying points of view can lead to conflict and pain. But God did not use the same mold when He created us, and He certainly never meant for us to live off by ourselves and serve Him independently. His purpose is to have us be together and to use our different personalities and gifts for the good of each other and the kingdom as a whole. As Proverbs 27:17 says, "As iron sharpens iron, so one person sharpens another."

The problem is that too often in our human nature we respond to others in ways other those that the King desires for His subjects—things like gossip, slander, always thinking we are right and insisting on our own way, harboring resentments and negative attitudes, being mean-spirited, cliquish, impatient, hard-hearted. The list could go on and on. This book will show us the care we can have for each other when, instead of doing what comes naturally to us in the flesh, we do what comes supernaturally to us by the Word of God and the Spirit of God working in our hearts.

This volume speaks of both the Kingdom of God and the church, and it may appear that the two terms are interchangeable. Indeed, they are related, so much so that what is written about relationships in the church applies also to the Kingdom. But they are not identical. As indicated earlier, the Kingdom of God is the everlasting, universal, eternal, all-inclusive kingdom of the great Creator in heaven. It goes from eternity to eternity. It includes all of God's creation: it includes all time, it includes all created matter. It includes all the things in heaven, the angel host. It includes all the things in earth, humanity. Psalm 103:19-22 gives an apt description. All things will be merged into the Kingdom of God, and 1 Corinthians 15:24-26 states the culmination of it: "Then comes the end, when He delivers the kingdom to God the Father, when He puts an end to all rule and all authority and power. For He must reign till He has put all enemies under His feet."

The church is a different entity. It is the body of Christ (Col. 1:18). The Kingdom of God is an invisible entity (Luke 17:20-21), but the church is the presence of our Lord visibly expressed in this age, in this time, in this dispensation. The church is the *ekklēsia*, the "called out" group in the earth (1 Cor. 1:2), and it has an assignment to preach the gospel around the world and to win the lost (Matt. 28:19-20).

Briefly stated, the Kingdom of God refers to the reign of God in the world. This kingdom is one that can never be destroyed and will never end. Its King, Jesus, will sit on the throne forever. The church is the people of God who live under Jesus' rule now, while waiting for the realization of God's kingdom in the future. The church is called to be witnesses to His kingdom, proclaiming God's message of salvation through Christ and demonstrating the power of the gospel so that others may be brought to live under God's reign.

I

THE KING'S DESIGN FOR KINGDOM LIVING

An astute and caring king desires that his subjects live in harmony and fellowship with each other. God created us so that we instinctively long for companionship, as evidenced by His declaration, "It is not good that man should be alone" (Gen. 2:18). God purposes order, and He has ordained that all living creatures come together "according to their kind." When He created the universe, God established certain basic laws, the aim of which is to foster proper relationships in society. The same is true of God's moral law, the intent of which is to guarantee the full expression of our freedom, not to stifle it.

Ideally, the laws of a community or a nation that regulate the lifestyles of its citizens are enacted to promote harmony and guard against confusion and discord. For example, I have a license that grants me the privilege of driving an automobile. However, in order to exercise that right, I have to meet certain conditions and drive under the restrictions of traffic regulations. I must observe speed laws, stop at red lights, drive in certain lanes, and yield at times to other vehicles. Suppose I don't want to submit to all these restrictions. Don't they constitute a violation of my liberties? After all, it's my car, and the state license guarantees me the right to operate it, and my taxes help pay for the road. Just for the sake of variety, perhaps I'll drive on the wrong side of the highway, against the flow of traffic. And why should I stop at red lights, wasting my valuable time waiting for the light to change? If I put such an attitude into practice, and every other driver did as he pleased, our privilege would quickly become a curse. True community, however, recognizes the mutual dependency of its members, the fulfillment of certain roles, and adherence to certain codes.

In the same way, our King desires that we enjoy the noblest relationships possible in the kingdom, and He has instituted guidelines to channel those relationships into a harmonious whole. We must never think of God as a severe tyrant who wants to restrict our freedom or to dampen our capacity to enjoy ourselves. The exact opposite is true. Everything in the Bible shows us how we can enjoy life on this earth to the very fullest, and if people lived in accord with the principles that God has ordained, then truly we would have heaven on earth. Our King has legislated against only those things that corrupt and destroy life and society (see Gal. 5:19-21), but He has decreed that "there is no law" against such things as the fruit of the Spirit, "love, joy, peace, longsuffering, kindness, goodness, faithfulness, gentleness, self-control" (Gal. 5:22-23).

The Tragedy of Loneliness

An old adage declares that solitude is the mother country of the strong, and certainly no life can ever be strong apart from its great silences and reflections and its self-communing and God-communing hours. But on the other hand, there are great qualities that thrive and develop only with the stimulating contact of mind with mind. A close friend of a distinguished statesman wrote in explanation of his failure, "He was the loneliest man I ever knew." The tragic collapse of a great financier, who took his own life, caused one of his associates to say, "His great fault was that he worked too much alone." The following lines offer us much to consider:

O crooked, lonely forest tree!
Yes, crooked because lonely.
How very different life would be
If only comrades two or three
Could share your lone monotony!

Our creator designed us to live in fellowship. He did not plan us to live in isolation as hermits and lone wolves. Our King made us so that we instinctively desire fellowship with Him and with each other. Without a relationship of love and trust and service with others, we become emotionally sick, growing miserable, frustrated and neurotic. The instinctive need for companionship that God instilled in us is graphically illustrated in the movie *Cast Away.* Chuck, a FedEx executive portrayed by Tom Hanks, survives a plane crash that leaves him stranded on a remote uninhabited Pacific island for four years. Although he manages to master the basic tools of survival with the help of some FedEx packages washed ashore from the crash, he feels the bitter despair of loneliness. While trying to start a fire by rubbing sticks together, Chuck cuts his hand. In a fury, he grabs a volleyball from one of the parcels and throws it. Upon retrieving the ball, he finds that his bloody hand has left an imprint on it. From that imprint he fashions a man's face and names it "Wilson," after the ball's manufacturer. Wilson becomes the companion that saves him from the wretchedness of isolation. Only in fellowship can we become what God created us to be.

The animal kingdom has an instinctive distrust of loneliness. When creatures gather into herds, flocks, packs and colonies, they are demonstrating the advantages of God's purpose in fellowship. Every individual animal in the group shares the value of the alertness, protective watchfulness, scent and sense of the entire group. During the hunt, wolves do not aimlessly run around their potential victim, yelping and howling. They have devised a strategic plan, which they carry out to perfection by constant communication. Each one understands his role and accepts the responsibility that the pack expects of him. This teamwork determines whether the pack lives or dies.

The same principle operates on the higher level of human life. The apostle Paul was teaching the incalculable advantages of fellowship when he wrote, "That you, being rooted and grounded in love, may be able to comprehend with all the saints . . ." (Eph. 3:17-18).

Satan's Sham

God doesn't want citizens of His Kingdom to be characterized by aloneness. He wills that we should have fellowship, and He has made ample provision to supply that basic need. However, Satan has alluring counterfeits in the world to provide a terrible substitute for the real thing. Never before have we had so many places of amusement and entertainment, but loneliness is still a major menace to life. The month of May is designated as "National Tavern Month" in America, and the promotion propaganda presents the neighborhood tavern as affording a cozy, congenial atmosphere for friendly fraternizing. Supposedly, "the month-long campaign marks the positive role that bars and taverns play in their communities." "Your neighborhood tavern is the friendliest place in town!" That slogan appeared in the headline of a special newspaper insert during National Tavern Month. The same edition of the newspaper carried six different articles describing brawls and murders that took place at taverns, and one article reporting the rape of a woman by a man she met at a bar. And that's the friendliest place in town?

Regardless of what one may think of the claims of tavern owners, the popularity of the pub does succeed in portraying the fundamental human need for fellowship, which includes sympathy and conviviality. God put into the human heart a strong desire for companionship, to love and to be loved, to know and to be known, and for many lonely people the cozy bar seems to be the answer to their needs. And it's a sad truth that the bar may offer the best counterfeit one can find to the fellowship that Jesus wants the church to experience. The congenial camaraderie of the bar may be an imitation, dealing out drinks instead of grace and an atmosphere that encourages escapism rather than the courage to face reality, but it is a permissive and inclusive fellowship. You can't shock people within that accepting society. You can spill out your secrets, and nobody seems to be shocked and don't care who you are or what you have done. So for the price of a few beers, people can find some measure of understanding, compatibility and sympathy. The Lord wants His kingdom to be an atmosphere in which its citizens can find those same qualities.

The Neglect of Fellowship

Fellowship in the contemporary church has not nearly approximated the ideal set forth in the Bible. "Fellowship" is one of the most overworked and least understood words among Christians. We commonly speak of "going to church," as if attendance at a meeting in a building entails all that is involved in the meaning of "church." An elevator full of people is not a *group*; it is a *collection*. Regrettably, this description applies to many of our church services. We collect around a given purpose for a given amount of time, and then we disperse again until time for the next gathering.

In a day of big, impersonal institutions the church has become so rigid in its organized structure that the New Testament pattern is barely recognizable. In our very bigness people can feel friendless and unnoticed in a forest of anonymity. Our urban culture has become so properly sophisticated that we are politely closed to each other. In many of our churches if there were half as much fellowship of the Spirit as there is spicy gossip, there would be foretastes of heaven.

Right in our midst there are hearts hungry for genuine Christian fellowship to solace and strengthen them as they grapple with the complexities of modern life. Our churches are filled with people who outwardly seem to be content and at peace, but inwardly they are crying out for someone who will love them and listen to them as they pour out their confusion, frustration and guilt. Too many times they hesitate to share their deep needs, because everyone else seems to be so happy and content. How can they find the courage to admit to such a self-contented group that they have problems, especially if they question their spiritually and wonder what's wrong with them.

Congregation or Community

The Christian church is not just a congregation; it is a community of saints, but too often that communion is drastically inconspicuous. Ideally, we "members of one another" (Rom. 12:5), but actually, being all on one roll is far from "being like-minded, having the same love, being of one accord, of one mind" (Phil. 2:2). In many buildings known as churches, spiritually minded believers often cannot find family fellowship. The buildings house Sunday audiences rather than a family gathering of brothers and sisters who share a common redemption in Christ. Our local churches should be harmonious fellowships where perfect love casts out fear, but many of them are little more than religious depots or appointed meeting places that afford opportunities for social hobnobbing. The superficial social camaraderie that the word "fellowship" often denotes in churches today is no more supernatural than the weekly Rotary Club meeting. That kind of fellowship, which is distinctly less than the biblical meaning of the term, is easily duplicated in secular society. However, the rich, deep, full fellowship of the New Testament, as we shall see, is unique to the church of Jesus Christ and has no parallel in any secular institution.

The Cultivation of Fellowship

The story of Robinson Crusoe is a thrilling account of the kind of life a resourceful human being can lead in total isolation. However, Robinson Crusoe Christians fail to reach the ideal of discipleship that the New Testament presents. Christian fellowship is not an optional extra; it is an essential part of the Christian life.

Something dies in the solitude of isolated discipleship that would have gained strength and effectiveness in the community. The New Testament never speaks of the saint as an individual who grew saintly by living alone; it always speaks of "saints" in the group, for to be a Christian is to share the common life of the body of Christ.

As a man on the earth, Jesus hungered for human companionship as naturally as a man hungers for food. The sages of the world may prefer solitude to society, but those within whom the Spirit of Christ dwells seek the company of others of like experience. Christ broke down the barriers that usually divide human beings from one another—the prejudices of race, nationality, or class. By His death He destroyed enmities and built up a new community. As a result, the early Christians felt that they had become members of a new race, distinct from Jew and Gentile, yet embracing both. It was a new kind of kingdom, where there is neither Greek nor Jew, barbarian, Scythian, slave nor free, male nor female, but where all are one in Christ Jesus (Col. 3:11; Gal. 3:28). Being a part of this kingdom does not literally obliterate our racial, social, and sexual distinctions. Our skin pigmentation does not change, nor necessarily do our social and cultural practices, or the accent with which we speak. Furthermore, men remain men and women remain women. But now in Christ we are absolutely equal before God, irrespective of our race, rank, or sex. As we experience a humbling before the cross to see ourselves and each other as equally sinful and guilty, and thus equally dependent on His grace, we acknowledge the fact that we are reduced to the same level, and so we welcome one another without distinction or discrimination. In Christ, by virtue of our union with Him, we are brothers and sisters in the same family. "Now, therefore," declared Paul, "you are no longer strangers and foreigners, but fellow citizens with the saints and members of the household of God" (Eph. 2:19).

The Sharing of Experiences

The British mountaineer Sir Martin Conway wrote about the "charms of solitude," but he also confessed that the "visions of beauty die unless they are shared." No traveler sees all the landscape. Each single observer has his own range and quality of sight, his own degree of perception, and his own impression. When individuals share their experiences together, learning from the rest enriches each one.

The same principle is true concerning our knowledge and experience of Jesus Christ. Realizing that principle, Paul writes to Philemon, "I pray that you may be active in sharing your faith, so that you will have a full understanding of every good thing we have in Christ" (v.6 NIV). If we had only one of the four Gospels in the New Testament, we would miss much in our knowledge and understanding of Christ. All four share the same story, but they vary the emphasis and impressiveness of it. If we could see Christ as all other believers have seen Him, our comprehension of Him would grow enormously. Every individual Christian has had a unique experience with Christ, and thus each one has a story to share. We can never cease learning about Christ from the encounters of others with Him. One person is drawn to Christ by His mercy; another by His righteousness; another is impressed by His matchless love; and another testifies of the joy of Christ; and so the accounts continue in inexhaustible fashion. If all the various peoples of the earth could gather together and describe the impressiveness and appeal of Jesus Christ, we would marvel at how small our previous knowledge of Him was. Only by the communion of all witnesses to Christ do we arrive at any comprehension of His greatness. He grows upon us more and more with every testimony that we hear.

Christ is not our private possession, but our commonwealth, and we are to share Him. When God was preparing the early Methodists for the great work they were afterwards to do, John

Wesley wrote, concerning the "Holy Club" at Oxford, that they made known to one another the real condition of their heart. Personal testimony, the sharing of experience, is an essential feature of Christian fellowship. It does not mean telling everybody everything always; but it does mean a willingness, as directed by the Spirit, to tell our fellow Christians of our triumphs, our temptations, our problems, and sometimes, as we shall see, of our faults and sins.

Thus, every believer has the privilege of using his wisdom, his experience, his insight and his faith on behalf of the entire body. Paul makes this fact unmistakably plain in Ephesians 4:16: "From whom the whole body, joined and knit together by what every joint supplies, according to the effective working by which every part does its share, causes growth of the body for the edifying of itself in love." As every joint of the physical body has a function to fulfill, every member of the body of Christ has his peculiar responsibility. The Bible emphasizes this truth very clearly: "But the manifestation of the Spirit is given to each one for the profit of all" (1 Cor. 12:7). Every individual Christian has something essential to share with the entire body.

Members One of Another

The New Testament presents four factors that are necessary for the healthy life of a church: "And they continued steadfastly in the apostles' doctrine and fellowship, in the breaking of bread, and in prayers" (Acts 2:42). Most churches emphasize doctrine, prayers and communion, but far too often the apostolic is devalued or missing altogether. How far can a three-wheeled wagon go?

Jesus made Himself amazingly dependent upon His disciples. He wanted them beside Him. He poured His life into theirs in sympathy and love, in longing and desire. Sometimes He found them dull in understanding, slow of heart, selfish, ambitious, and earthbound. They often disappointed Him. They slept in His most troubled hour when He most wanted their wakeful comradeship. When danger threatened Him they scattered from His side and fled into fearful hiding. And when His enemies condemned Him to be marched out to the place of execution, there was not one of them present to take an end of the cross with Him, or even to comfort Him with their nearness. Yet, He always made them believe that He could not do without them. Finally, His patience prevailed over their slowness. His love purged them of their faults and weaknesses, and they became the foundations of His kingdom. They were transformed by His fellowship.

One of the great yearnings of the Lord for His disciples was that they might cultivate an intimate fellowship, as evidenced by His repeated emphasis on loving one another. He knew how much the world would be impressed by their mutual love and unity. The apostle Paul had a similar passion. He reminded believers that a common act of grace had raised them up together and made them sit together in heavenly places in Christ Jesus, and that by the same mercy all enmities and hatreds and suspicion s were abolished (Eph. 2). And when he warned them to put away lying and to speak truth, it was because "we are members of one another" (Eph. 4:25). There is no private sin, no isolated wrong. A lie is a sin against the brotherhood, a hurt inflicted upon others.

This idea of fellowship dominates the New Testament teachings concerning the church. Therefore, any thought of enjoying salvation or being a Christian in isolation is foreign to the New Testament.

II

THE BOND OF UNITY

Generally speaking, the contemporary church has devalued the biblical meaning of fellowship to mean nothing more than a congenial social gathering, such as a church supper or picnic. Such associations are good and proper, and they have a distinct place in the lives of Christians, because God created our social nature as well as our spiritual nature. But we fall far short of the deeper meaning of fellowship as taught in the New Testament when we regard our social functions as the climax of all fellowship. With that concept, skating parties, picnics and other activities that we enjoy in group association become the end instead of the by-product of true fellowship.

Before attempting to define the biblical word translated "fellowship," we must understand that there is a boundary outside of which genuine fellowship is impossible. The boundary of all harmonious relationships is love, a word that suggests dozens of related terms that describe attitudes necessary for the experience of true fellowship—such qualities as concern, compassion, trust, hospitality, sharing, forgiveness, to name only a few. The new life of the Christian involves more than a personal and private relationship to Jesus, to be lived in isolation. John Wesley declared, "To turn Christianity into a solitary religion is to destroy it." It's true that every believer is personally related to Christ, but to restrict Christianity to individual relationships to Him without a relationship to one another is to make it hopelessly lopsided. "Lone wolf" Christianity (or should I say "lone sheep" Christianity?) is not biblical Christianity.

The Corporate Nature of the Kingdom

God has not designed His kingdom to be inhabited by independent souls, but as a family of redeemed individuals who are keenly aware that they belong together. It's true that we have an individual relationship to Christ, just as an individual branch abides in the vine. But it's also true that our relationship to Christ has a corporate aspect as well, for all the branches are members of the same vine. The church of God is a family in which we are all brothers and sisters, a kingdom in which we are fellow-citizens, and the body of Christ of which He is the head and we are the members. We are also sheep in the same flock under the same shepherd. A building is made of individual bricks, but the bricks are not suspended in the air without any connection to one other; they are cemented together. It is impossible to escape from the reality that we cannot belong to Christ without thereby belonging to His people as well. The entire New Testament emphasizes this twofold relationship and the interdependence of the dual fellowship. We cannot be rightly related to each other unless we are rightly related to God, but conversely we cannot be rightly related to God unless we are rightly related to each other. These two fellowships affect each other—the one with God cementing the other, and the one with our brothers and sisters reflecting the other. There is no such thing as fellowship of believers among themselves apart from their individual fellowship with God; and there is no fellowship with God that does not produce as its primary and characteristic result a living fellowship with other believers.

Love Is a Command, Not an Option

A vital part of life in the Spirit is life with each other. The New Testament is filled with exhortations to walk in the Spirit or to be filled with the Spirit. If you examine the passages that record those exhortations, you will find that almost every one includes instruction concerning mutual relationships between those who are doing the walking or who are filled. See, for example, Galatians 5:25–6:10 and Ephesians 5:18–6:9. Love is the first fruit of the Spirit, and according to the apostle Paul, it's far more important than any of the gifts and ministries of the Spirit, or all of them put together. He wrote that if we have been endowed with all spiritual gifts, even of the most spectacular kind, if we have been endowed with all knowledge and all faith, even if we have done heroic deeds up to martyrdom, but if we have no love, we don't gain anything. In fact, he says, we are precisely nothing in the sight of God (see 1 Cor. 13:1-3).

We have no option in the matter of loving our brothers and sisters in the family of God. We have no liberty in choosing to love or not to love our fellow citizens as the mood strikes us. In various forms, the New Testament repeatedly gives the command to love one another. 2 Peter 2:17 instructs us to "honor all people," having a general respect for them as creatures carrying the image of God, but specifically the verse commands us to "love the brotherhood." The desired intimacy within the family is not possible outside the circle of divine love. Paul reminded the Thessalonian Christians that God had taught them to love one another, and although they were practicing that command toward all their fellow believers in Macedonia, he urged them to excel even more (1 Thess. 4:9-10).

Jesus spent the final hours before His betrayal gathered with His closest followers in the Upper Room, where He instituted the Lord's Supper and revealed to them, in the form of teaching and prayer, His deepest concerns in that hour of crisis. If we liken the New Testament to the temple, John 13-17 is certainly the inner sanctuary of the temple. As we read those chapters, we enter into the very mind of Christ as He revealed to the apostles His innermost thoughts about His imminent departure and the coming of The Holy Spirit to replace Him, about His own return at the end to take His people to Himself, and about the responsibilities of kingdom citizens during the interim period between His departure and His return. It is extremely significant that as Jesus gave these instructions, He was completely aware of the fact that He would have no further opportunity to teach His apostles before His death. What did He consider to be the most important things to tell those who were to continue His work? Do you recall the last command He gave them? It was not that they be great fund-raisers, or great propagandists, or even great soul winners. It was simply that they love one another, a charge that He considered to be so important that He gave it explicitly on that occasion three times (13:34; 15:12, 17) and implicitly many other times.

The fact that Jesus commanded us to love one another makes it certain that love is not optional. Some may protest that love is not a fit subject for commandments, because it is an emotion, something you cannot control, something over which you have no power, and something that you may not have even invited into your life. So it seems perfectly reasonable to ask the question, "How can you command me to start loving someone I don't love or stop loving someone I do love? I have no control over the matter. It happens or it doesn't happen. I'm at love's command; love is not at my command."

Such an attitude betrays a faulty understanding of the true nature of love. We can be assured that our King doesn't give commands that cannot be obeyed. The very fact that He commanded us to love one another (in Matthew 5:44 our enemies as well) tells us that there is a love that is not the victim of our emotions, but the servant of our wills. Love is not uncontrollable passion. It's not primarily how you feel; it's what you do. Love involves choice and conduct.

What Kind of Love?

The reason that people are so confused is that English has one word for love, whereas the Greek language, in which the New Testament was written, uses several words for love. For example, the word *eros* describes the type of love found in romantic relationships between a man and a woman. The word *philia* describes the type of love found in strong friendships, involving affection and mutual support. The word *storge* describes the type of love found in family relationships, and it involves empathy, affection, and compassion.

The kind of love Kingdom citizens are to display toward one another is described by the word *agape*, which the Christian faith adopted and to which it gave a deeper meaning and more significant application. Apart from about twenty references in the Greek translation of the Old Testament, the word is rarely found in secular literature before the New Testament. The reason is not difficult to find, because the world regarded the word to represent a weak, servile, ignoble character. *Agape* means an active seeking of the highest good of the other person, even when that love is unrequited, or even met with bitter and rude rebuff. The basic meaning of the word shows that in obedience to the command of Christ we can deliberately set our love on people whom we don't naturally like, even if we don't feel like loving them.

Agape is really God-like love. Why does God love you? It certainly isn't because of your intrinsic worth or your sterling character or you charitable deeds. Basically, God loves because His very nature is love (1 John 4:8), but in addition, there is a fundamental logic to His love. Long ago Moses explained it to the people of Israel, recorded in Deuteronomy 7:7-8. He discounted the possibility that God loved them because they deserved it or because they were greater than any other nation. The true reason is the simple logic of divine love: God loves you because He loves you. The only explanation of the love of God is the love of God. In other words, God's love is not aroused by the worth of its object, but only by itself.

Am I Commanded to Love You?

The Bible clearly teaches that we are to love others with God's love. The character of that kind of love will not allow us to restrict our love to the select few that we include in our inner circle, that is, those of whom we are really fond or with whom we have some natural affinity. Luke 10:25-37 records the conversation between Jesus and an expert in the law regarding loving your neighbor as yourself. The teacher of the law asked, "Who is my neighbor?" In posing that question, the shortsighted legalist was actually setting limits on his love. In effect he was saying that there were some people undeserving of his goodwill. In response, Jesus gave the parable of the Good Samaritan, illustrating the vast difference between genuine *agape* and the expert's rigid and narrow interpretation of God's love. If I love "with the affection of Jesus Christ" (Phil. 1:8), I will not consider your looks, your wealth, or any other such quality as a requisite for my love. There is only one consideration—if you are my brother or sister, then I am to seek your good actively because I am commanded to do it. In fact, Jesus taught us to love our enemies, to do good to them, to bless them, to pray for them (Luke 6:27-28). True love serves those who don't deserve to be served. If we practice the love of Jesus, then we will not give others what they deserve, but we will give them what they need.

How We Are To Love

The command of Jesus to love is not vague and undefined, but quite precise. He said that we are to love each other **as He has loved us** (John 13:34; 15:12). He described His command as "new," and His own example is what makes it new. No longer are we to follow the pattern of the world and love only those who love us. Nor are we merely to follow the dictates of the old commandment and love our neighbors as ourselves (if most of us did that much, wouldn't we be madly in love with our neighbors?). The newness of the command of Jesus is that we are to love others just as He loved us, which goes far beyond mere sentiment or emotion all the way to sacrificial service.

Do you recall where Jesus was when He issued the command to love? And do you remember what the disciples were doing as they entered that Upper Room? We would think that their affection for their Master would cause them to give Him needed encouragement in the hour of His greatest crisis. Surely their close friendship would lead them to offer mutual support for each other. Unfortunately, that wasn't the atmosphere at all. Instead of affording one another the benefit of mutual encouragement and giving strength to Jesus, they were bickering and arguing about which one of them was the greatest (Luke 22:24). In the midst of their wrangling, Jesus instructed them concerning the proper role and attitude of a true leader. He taught that service and humility are the qualities of genuine leadership, and He pointed to Himself as the example they should follow.

In those days it was customary for the host at a meal to provide a servant to wash the dusty feet of his guests. But on this occasion there was no servant available to perform such an ignoble act. Perhaps Jesus waited to see if one of the apostles would volunteer to be the servant of the others and was their feet. If He did, He waited in vain. Instead of assuming the role of a servant, they were lording themselves over one another in petty competition. I can imagine what the reaction would have been if Jesus suggested that one of them do the dirty work. There certainly would not have been a rush to see who could be the first to grab a towel and a washbasin. I think that most of the group would have turned to John with the suggestion, "All right, Johnny, you're the youngest in the crowd. Now show a little respect for your elders and wash our feet." Or perhaps they would have looked at Matthew with the righteous comment, "Well, Levi, you're the biggest sinner among us. You cheated us at the tax table, so make atonement by washing our feet." But it could be that when Jesus announced that somebody needed to act as foot washer, all eyes would automatically focus on Peter. "All right, Rocky, you're the one. You're always shooting off your mouth, so now is the opportunity to put a little action to your words." The painful fact is that every one of them would have found ample reason why someone else should do the work, and they would have perfectly satisfied at being waited on hand and foot. But not a one of them was willing to do the menial task himself. After all, they were apostles, not waiters. They were masters, not servants! Their attitude betrayed the fact that they had not yet learned the lesson that prompted Paul's exhortation to the Galatians some years later: "Through love serve one another" (Gal. 5:13).

As a result of their insensitive and selfish attitude, their feet were unwashed. Then, after supper had begun, Jesus took it upon Himself to do what none of them had been willing to do. He became their servant and washed their feet, thereby acting out a parable that teaches the truth that genuine love issues in service. Of what value is it to claim to love people in a vague and general and diffuse way? Love is always active and expresses itself in concrete acts of goodness.

In 1878, not long after General Booth had formed the Salvation Army, a prominent American Methodist minister, Samuel Logan Brengle, who had aspirations of being a bishop, was particularly enamored with the idea of a great worldwide movement such as that envisaged by General Booth. His vision was so strong that he left a fine pastorate and traveled to England to join the Salvation Army. At first, Booth was reluctant to accept Brengle's services, because he recognized a spirit of pride upon him. "You've been your own boss too long," the general declared. When Brengle persisted, Booth, in order to instill humility in him, put him to work shining the boots of the other enlistees. At first Brengle reacted in indignation. "Have I followed my own fancy across the Atlantic in order to black boots?" he asked himself. Suddenly, there flashed before his mind a vision of Jesus bending over the dirty, smelly feet of rough, unlettered fishermen. "Lord," he whispered, "You washed their feet; I will black their boots." Brengle went on to become the first American-born commissioner of the Salvation Army.

Immediately following the washing of feet, Jesus explained to His disciples that He had given them an example and that they should do likewise (see John 13:12-17). It was not beneath the dignity of the King to garb Himself as a slave, get down on His knees and humble Himself in the service of others. Is it beneath ours? Christ expressed the ultimate of His love in John 15:13: "Greater love has no one than this, than to lay down one's life for his friends." True love always gives in order to serve; it sacrifices itself in order to serve others. Following the example of our Lord does not mean that we are to wait for the opportunity to perform heroic deeds of self-sacrifice, for life is full of opportunities for lesser sacrifices. Here is love in homespun—the doing of the little things, the giving of the cup of cold water in the name of Jesus (Matt. 10:42), the small touches that can mean so much. John asked, "But whoever has this world's goods, and sees his brother in need, and shuts up his heart from him, how does the love of God abide in him?" (1 John 3:17).

Paul commended the believers at Thessalonica for their labor prompted by love (1 Thess. 1:3). Love leads to labor on behalf of others; otherwise, it isn't real. It's mere sentimentality. There is a great deal of sentiment in love, but it doesn't stop there. The true assessment of the quality of love isn't in what we say, but in what it leads us to do. The Bible tells us that love is kind (1 Cor. 13:4), and kindness is serving one another.

How Long Must I Love You?

With the vivid and commanding example of Christ's love, the expectation concerning our love is quite clear: "By this we know love, because He laid down His life for us. And we also ought to lay down our lives for the brethren" (1 John 3:16). We do not serve our fellow citizens by dying for them as Jesus did on the cross, but we do serve them in living for them, as He did in His life. There is an interesting grammatical feature in John's statement that strongly declares the type of love we are to display. In stating that Christ "laid down" His life, John used a tense that signifies that He did it once and for all, at a specific moment in time (see Heb. 10:12). However, in exhorting us to "lay down our lives for the brethren," John changes to the present tense. The significance is that while Jesus gave the ultimate display of love in His once-for-all death, we are engaged in a continual process of showing our love. Love's obligation to the brethren is never finished; we serve as long as there is need. As we will see shortly, 1 Corinthians 13:4 declares that love suffers long, that is, we don't get impatient with others and give up on them. *Agape* love is steadfast.

Is It Real?

In 2 Corinthians 6:4-6, Paul listed several qualities by which we commend ourselves as servants of God. One of the characteristics he mentions in verse 6 is love, which he describes as "sincere." The word is literally "non-hypocritical," or in a more positive sense, genuine (see Rom. 12:9). We might wonder why Paul felt the need to add such a word when writing about the kind of love that Christians are to have for one another. He needed to talk about a non-pretending love because there is a poor substitute for love not uncommon among Christians. It is an artificial pretense, a superficial *bon ami* in which there is no genuine care and compassion.

That kind of love is well illustrated in the letter that a man received from the manager of a large department store. The man had written a letter of complaint, and in response the manager dictated a letter of apology. Unfortunately, however, the secretary hit a wrong key at a strategic point. As a result, here is what the irate customer read: "We are very sorry indeed to receive your complaint, because we assure you that although we have tens of thousands of customers, we fake a personal interest in each one." Perhaps that statement more accurately describes our interest in others than we want to admit.

I find it to be a sad truth that many Christians find it easier to love at a distance than close at hand. It's much more convenient to express concern for someone in Africa or some other faraway place than nearby, where we may have to get involved in costly time and service. It's also a sad truth that many people find it easier to give money to prove their love than to give themselves—their time, energy and personal effort. We often find it easier to be enthusiastic about Humanity with a capital "H" than it is to love individuals, especially those who are not attractive, adventurous, intellectual, or are otherwise uninteresting. Could it be that a declaration of loving everybody in general is nothing more than a limp excuse for loving nobody in particular?

Learning to Love

Only by the love that sacrifices and serves will people recognize that we are Christ's disciples (John 13:35), because it's only by such love that we shall bear the likeness of Christ. In fact, I believe that it would not be an exaggeration to say that if there is no humble service in our lives, nothing comparable to Christ's washing of the apostles' feet, we can hardly qualify as disciples of Jesus. He Himself stated that a disciple is not above his teacher, nor a servant above his lord (see John 13:13-16).

Without this Christ-like love, fellowship in the Kingdom of God will be patently superficial, and the Kingdom citizens will remain in the selfish isolation of individual concerns. In John 12:24 Jesus said, "Unless a grain of wheat falls into the ground and dies, it remains alone." Self-preservation, then, is the *cause* of loneliness. Jesus then added, "But if it dies, it produces much grain." Self-sacrifice, then, is the *cure* of loneliness.

The early Christians learned well the lessons that Jesus taught on love, and they cemented their fellowship in the midst of a hostile, persecuting, jeering world. In his *Apology*, written near the end of the second century, the Christian apologist Tertullian provides one of the earliest descriptions of post-biblical Christianity. In Chapter xxxix of that treatise, he gives vivid details of how Christians actively served one another. "It is the exercise of this sort of love," he wrote, that was the chief "brand" of Christians. The pagans, however, thought it was foolish to subordinate your own interests and concerns to those of other people. Tertullian wrote of the pagan reaction to the example of the Christians: "'See,' say they, 'how they love each other'; for they themselves hate each other: and 'see how ready they are to die for each other'; for they themselves are more ready to slay each other." I wonder if Tertullian would write similar words if he surveyed the contemporary Christian scene. The church is a fellowship of redeemed sinners, born of the Spirit of God, and as such it is a supernatural community. But it can only reveal its true nature as a divine society when it is characterized by divine love. After all, "love . . . is the bond of perfection" (Col. 3:14).

Christianity would present a lovely and attractive sight to the world if those who profess it were more actuated and animated by this divine principle, and if they paid a due regard to the command on which Christ placed so much emphasis.

But how can we learn so great a lesson? Only by practice. Looking at pictures doesn't make one an artist, and listening to music doesn't make one a musician. The paints must be mixed, and the instruments must be played. In like manner, we can love in no other way than by loving.

Summary Description of Love

It's beyond question that the key to Kingdom relationships is love. Indeed, it is the mark of spiritual maturity, as the apostle Paul emphasized in 1 Corinthians 13. In a brief paragraph, verses 4-7, he lists ten qualities of the love that Kingdom citizens are to display. The first characteristic is *steadfastness.* Verse 4 states, "Love suffers long," that is, it enables us to be patient with others. Sometimes we get aggravated with people and give up on them and say, "I'm through with them. They don't deserve my love." One Peanuts cartoon strip shows Lucy standing with her arms folded and a stern expression on her face. Charlie Brown pleads, "Lucy, you must be more loving. This world really needs love. You have to let yourself love to make this world a better place." Lucy angrily whirls around and knocks Charlie Brown to the ground. She screams at him, "Look, Blockhead, the world I love. It's people I can't stand." But the love that suffers long is totally unconditional. It's choosing to love people not because of who they are, but n spite of who they are and in spite of what they may have done to you. The moment we quit loving people who offend or irritate us, we become unlike the Lord Jesus. The Bible tells us in John 13:1 that Jesus loved His disciples "to the end." True love is long-suffering. It forgives 70x7 and then keeps on forgiving.

The second quality listed in verse 4 is that love is *kind.* The word comes from a root that means to be useful, to be helpful, or to be suitable. Sometimes it's translated goodness, tenderness, friendliness, or generosity. What all that tells us is that kindness is love in action. It's attitude translated into practical action. In other words, love involves serving others. Kindness is a powerful medicine for a hurting world. Stephen Grellet, a Quaker missionary in the early nineteenth century, wrote, "I shall pass through this world but once. Any good thing, therefore, that I can do, or any kindness that

I can show to any human being, let me do it now. Let me not defer it or neglect it, for I shall not pass this way again." Mark Twain called kindness "a language that the deaf can hear and the blind can read." Kindness is a universal language, for it does not speak to the intellect, but directly to the heart.

The third quality, again in verse 4, is negative. *Love does not envy.* Love does not begrudge the gifts that others have; rather, love rejoices when good things happen to other people. You cannot love someone and envy that person at the same time, because love is glad for what the other person has. There is no rivalry or competition in love. If I want something that you have, it means that I don't rejoice that you have it. And if I don't rejoice that you have it, it's because I don't sincerely love you. Envy is a poison that eventually consumes the person who harbors it in his heart. Proverbs 14:30 says that envy is as the rottenness of the bones.

Verse 4 lists the fourth quality of love, which is also negative. "Love does not parade itself, is not puffed up." That means that *love is not arrogant*. Love is not boastful. It doesn't swagger. If I love you, I don't look down on you and rejoice that I have more than you. The Greek word for "parade" means to exaggerate or display yourself, to brag about yourself. Literally, it means to be a windbag, to talk in such a manner that you call attention to yourself. The word translated "puffed up" means to inflate. It's the act of puffing yourself up in your own eyes until you feel so superior to others that you cannot possibly love them. Pride and love cannot dwell in the same heart. You cannot be big-headed and big-hearted at the same time, because boasting is being concerned with yourself, while love is being concerned with others.

Verse 5 tells us that *love does not behave rude*ly. The term means to act with bad manners, to act dishonorably, to be overbearing, to be insensitive to others. It's the opposite of being polite and courteous. You see rudeness every day. It's the person who elbows his way through and cuts into the line. It's the person who interrupts and talks over others. It's the person who spoils a pleasant gathering with his uproarious laughter and speech. It's the inconsiderate person with the attitude, "I'll do whatever I want, and if you don't like it, tough!" Love says, "I will do whatever ministers to others, and if I don't like it, tough." A person who is rude is a person who is unloving and unlike the Lord Jesus Christ, who was meek and gentle, and who thought of others first.

The sixth characteristic, presented in verse 5, is that *love is self-denying*. Godly love doesn't say, "Me first! I know my rights!" The person who loves puts his responsibilities above his rights. When you became a citizen of the Kingdom of God, you lost all your rights. What rights does a dead person have? You were crucified with Christ. You were bought with a price, and you are not your own. You belong to the King. Your rights have now become His rights, and He has commanded you to love. He Himself has set the example that we are to follow, because He did not seek that which was His own, but freely gave up His all for us (see 2 Cor. 8:9; Mark 10:45). Love does not use people to gain its own advantage. It looks outward rather than inward. It heeds the admonition of Philippians 2:3-4: "Let nothing be done through selfish ambition or conceit, but in lowliness of mind let each esteem others better than himself. Let each of you look out not only for his own interests, but also for the interests of others."

The seventh quality, found in verse 5, is that *love is not provoked.* It's not touchy, ready to explode like a shotgun with a hair trigger. Some people seem to be covered with buttons, and the slightest bump of the wrong button sets off an instant reaction of explosive anger. The reason for that outburst is that the love of the Lord is not there. If you really want to know what you're full of, just look at what spills out when someone pushes your button. Your temper is a sign of what is in our heart. A bad temper is something you never lose by losing, and it's always a symptom of an unloving spirit. Some people excuse their bad temper by saying, "Sure, I may lose my temper now and then, but it's all over in a few minutes." A nuclear bomb is also over in seconds. A great deal of damage can be done in a very short time. True love is serene, not easily angered or quick-tempered.

The eighth mark of love, again in verse 5, is that *love thinks no evil.* The word used here is actually a bookkeeping term, meaning to keep an account. Love doesn't keep a record of faults. It's not a collector of grudges. Being easily angered is a quick reaction that results in hurtful words and harmful actions. Keeping a record of wrongs is the long-term decision to hold on to bitterness and resentment, to choose not to forgive. The one is a quick flaring up, and the other is a slow burn. There are some people who would make great archaeologists, because they're so good at digging up the past. Love does not keep a ledger of wrongs committed against it. It buries those things in the grave of God's forgetfulness. When it comes to grievances, love has a bad memory. When we repent, God forgives all offenses and keeps no records (see Psalm 130:3-4; Jer. 31:34).

Verse 6 states the ninth quality. *Love does not rejoice in iniquity, but rejoices in the truth.* The negative statement about iniquity means two things. First, it means that love takes no pleasure in unrighteousness, injustice, and wickedness. Love never rejoices when God is dishonored and His law is disobeyed. This word is particularly appropriate for modern society. There are certain practices that were once abhorrent to people.There was even legislation against them. Then people began to overlook these evils and tolerate them. Over a period of time the evils were legalized. Then the evils were promoted. Then the evils were celebrated. Now there is persecution against those who still call those things evil. Society tells us that love means putting away all concepts of sin and iniquity and to be completely accepting of whatever someone wants to do. But this is not true love at all. Rather than rejoicing, love cries out, "Rivers of water run down from my eyes, because men do not keep Your law" (Psalm 119:136). How can we rejoice in the kind of things that made it necessary for the Lord Jesus to die on the cross?

The statement about not delighting in evil also means that love does not rejoice when evil befalls someone else. Love is never glad at another person's misfortune, never gossips about another's problems. People who gossip rejoice when somebody does wrong. They hear a secret and can't wait to tell it. Love doesn't overlook sin in others. Instead, it deals with sin according to the instructions of Galatians 6:1: "Brethren, if a man is overtaken in any trespass, you who are spiritual restore such a one in a spirit of gentleness, considering yourself lest you also be tempted." Before we share anything about others, we should ask three questions. One, is it true? Two, even if it is true, is it necessary to tell it? Some things that are true are better not told. Three, is it kind? Our motive should be restorative.

The positive statement about rejoicing in the truth belongs together with the preceding negative statement, serving as its contrast. We must love and practice biblical truth at all costs. The world would have us to overlook evil for the sake of love, but nowhere in the Bible can you find such a compromise between love and evil. It's a watered-down Christian love that approves immoral behavior and believes false teachings in the name of love, in complete disregard of biblical principles of morality and rejection of biblical doctrinal truths. How can we lovingly approve a lifestyle which God in his Word condemns and how can we compromise biblical truth with falsehood? We must love people, but not soft-pedal sin and dilute the purity of biblical teachings? Balancing truth and love is never easy. It often involves confrontation, but sometimes truly loving someone requires loving confrontation.

Verse 7 provides numbers ten through thirteen in the list of love's qualities. *Love bears all things.* The word "bears" comes from the Greek word for "roof." It means "to protect by covering over," just as a roof provides a protective covering from the elements.

This covering supports what is placed upon it and covers what is placed underneath it.

Love acts in both ways in bearing all things. Love protects what is within by guarding against resentment, anger, and discouragement. Love doesn't point out every fault or shortcoming. Love doesn't complain, quibble, or criticize. Love doesn't expose, exploit, gloat, or condemn. Rather than dwelling on shortcomings, love chooses to put everything in the hands of God.

Love is also a roof that protects against the storms of life, just as the roof of a house protects against physical storms. Love stands up under the weight of adverse circumstances, bears the pressures, faces the trials, and does not give up. Love is a shelter from compromising situations and defamatory speech, a defense against temptation. Real *agape* love is always there in times of trouble to lend support.

Number 11 in the descriptive list of love is that *love believes all things.* That statement does not mean that love is gullible, stupid, naive, or blind. Nor does it mean that love ignores problems and challenges. Love sees everything—the beautiful and the ugly, the good and the bad—but it chooses to look beyond the problems and conflicts and to see the best in every situation. The Greek word translated "believe" is the same word for faith or trust. The verb means to put your faith or trust in someone or something. Love does not believe an obvious lie or blindly put its trust in untrustworthy people. But love chooses to believe the best about people until proven otherwise. When we truly love someone, we believe the best about them, and we whole-heartedly believe in what God can do for them, even when they struggle and fail. Before He went to the cross, Jesus knew that Peter would fail and would deny Him. In spite of that knowledge, Jesus said to Peter: "Simon, Simon! Indeed, Satan has asked for you, that he may sift you as wheat. But I have prayed for you, that your faith should not fail; and when you have returned to Me, strengthen your brethren" (Luke 22:31-32). We should love each other with that "never-give-up" kind of belief.

The twelfth feature of love is that *love hopes all things.* In the English language we think of hope as wishful or optimistic thinking, without any assurance that whatever we hope for will happen. However, in the Bible "hope" means such a sure and confident expectation that we anticipate seeing the manifestation of our hope. True *agape* love doesn't assume failure or a bad result in someone's life, but rather remembers the power of Jesus to transform lives, and 'hopes' all things with a sure and confident expectation.

The thirteenth quality of love is that *love endures all things.* The word translated "endures" literally means "to stay under." It's a refusal to budge when the going gets tough. It's the attitude of a person who is not going to surrender to defeat, regardless of what comes against him. When applied to love, it means that we don't give up and quit loving when it's difficult to love. We remain true to our commitment and stay faithful. True love continues in the face of rejection and opposition, insult and injury. Love perseveres because it's unconditional and chooses to love people in spite of themselves.

The list ends with the concise but forceful declaration, "Love never fails!" Does that statement mean that you don't really love God if you ever sin? If that's the case, then how many of us could truthfully claim to love God. Did Peter really love the Lord, having failed Him? Does the statement mean that you have never really loved a person if you failed to give needed support? Does it mean that a child who disobeys his parents doesn't really love them? The Greek word for fail is *pipto,* which literally means "to fall down," with the thought that something that falls down perishes, or comes to an end. The entire context of 1 Corinthians 13 declares the superiority of love over spiritual gifts. Verse 8 declares the permanency of love in contrast to the transitory nature of gifts.

The Amplified Bible translates the verse as follows: "Love never fails [never fades out or becomes obsolete or comes to an end]. As for prophecy (the gift of interpreting the divine will and purpose), it will be fulfilled and pass away; as for tongues, they will be destroyed and cease; as for knowledge, it will pass away [it will lose its value and be superseded by truth]." The New Living Translation says, "Love will last forever, but prophecy and speaking in unknown languages and special knowledge will all disappear." Phillips offers the following graphic translation: "It is, in fact, the one thing that still stands when all else has fallen. For if there are prophecies they will be fulfilled and done with, if there are "tongues" the need for them will disappear, if there is knowledge it will be swallowed up in truth."

This word "fail"describes a quality of love that is enduring and everlasting. It is the opposite of being transitory and fleeting. The Bible makes it emphatically clear that God's love for us will never fail. Nothing can separate us from the love of God. This is the kind of love we are called to have, a love that will never come to an end. In a later chapter we will offer further comments on some of the qualities of love that we have discussed and explore additional characteristics presented elsewhere in the New Testament.

III

PARTNERS

As we most frequently use the word "fellowship" today, we are describing a subjective feeling, an experience or a consciousness of belonging together. For example, we talk about the great fellowship we had at a church supper or retreat, meaning that we enjoyed each other's company. The dining facilities in most church buildings is called the "Fellowship Hall," suggesting that this is the designated place where people gather to enjoy fellowship. That kind of chumminess is both good and desirable, and we certainly should feel a special affinity toward others in our group. However, if our idea of fellowship is limited to genial social activities, whether inside or outside the church building, then we have fallen drastically short of fellowship in the biblical sense. In the New Testament "fellowship" is very much an objective fact, rather than a simple subjective feeling.

There are several words in the New Testament that express the basic idea of "fellowship." The root of all of them is the word *koinos*, which means "common." Growing out of this word are the nouns *koinonia* ("fellowship," "communion") and *koinonos* ("partner"), and the verb *koinoneo* ("to share"). Each of the words contains the idea of sharing something in common with someone. This group of words always describes a common interest between individuals, and a mutual and active pursuit of that interest in harmony with each other.

This meaning is well illustrated in the use of the words in everyday Greek society. In secular Greek *koinonia* described a close and intimate friendship in at least three areas. First, it was the usual word to describe a business partnership. Even today in the modern Greek language, the word *koinonos* is almost exclusively a business term in its secular usage. A second use of the word was as a term for marriage. Ancient literature describes two people entering into marriage in order to have *koinonia* of life, that is, to live together a life in which they share everything. A third use, even among pagans, was to describe a person's relationship to deity. For example, Epictetus, a Stoic philosopher of the first century, spoke of the aim of religion as "to have *koinonia* with Zeus."

The use of these words in the New Testament shows that the fellowship in which the Kingdom community should participate is just as wide and far-reaching as that shown by the words in secular Greek. A study of the various passages in the New Testament that use the words reveals that our common share in Kingdom privilege and responsibility is threefold. The Kingdom of God consists of people who have all had the same experience, who participate in a co-operative service, and who have reciprocal responsibilities.

A Common Experience

As I have already stated, the fundamental idea of the word *koinonia* is that of something held in common. Therefore, in the Kingdom community, the first and foremost meaning of fellowship is that it speaks of something that we **share in** together. We have all experienced a new birth and the Holy Spirit indwells each one of us to enable us to live a life of obedience and holiness and to transform us into the likeness of our King. A shared faith (Titus 1:4), a shared grace (Phil. 1:7) and a shared salvation (Jude 3) are the roots of *koinonia.* Each individual Christian has been **saved** by **grace** through **faith** (Eph. 2:8), and it is this common experience that makes us one. A graphic illustration of this fact is found in Philemon 17, where Paul appeals to Philemon to show mercy to the runaway slave Onesimus, who is now a new brother in the faith. He bases the appeal on the shared experience that has united the three—apostle, master and slave are now partners (*koinonoi*).

The vital and impressive Kingdom fellowship that we see in the New Testament is extraordinarily unique, and it cannot be duplicated in any other community. Here is Saul of Tarsus, once a haughty Pharisee, Hebrew of the Hebrews, who was passionately dedicated to Jewish tradition and law. Before he entered the Kingdom of God, he looked with contempt upon poor illiterate slaves from Greek slums—barbarians, he once would have called them, Scythians, miserable outsiders. Now he miraculously regards them as his brothers and shares his deepest intimacies with them. Only the supernatural experience of a new birth could account for such a radical change of attitude. Imagine a Christian love-feast in the catacombs, and a Roman lady, with imperial blood in her veins, a kinswoman of the Caesars, taking the cup from the hand of a nameless waif of the streets, and both of them feeling it was the most natural thing in the world to do, for there was a love deeper than sisterhood between them now. Once again the only explanation is that of the common experience of a new birth.

Fellowship with God the Father

In no earthly kingdom do common citizens experience the intimate relationship with royalty that is a vital feature of the Kingdom of God. All three persons of the Trinity are involved in our common experience of saving grace. The apostles have clearly stated that their purpose in bearing witness to us is that we might have fellowship with them, "and truly our fellowship is with the Father and with His Son Jesus Christ" (1 John 1:3). In other words, our fellowship with each other arises from and rests on our fellowship with God. When fellowship with God is disrupted by disobedience, fellowship with one another breaks down. Conversely, when we maintain fellowship with God as we "walk in the light," we enjoy fellowship with one another (1 John 1: 6-7).

Fellowship with God the Son

Next, God has called us "into the fellowship of His Son, Jesus Christ our Lord" (1 Cor. 1:9). This statement is in connection with Paul's teaching that while we are "eagerly waiting for the revelation of our Lord Jesus Christ," a faithful God "will also confirm (us) to the end, that (we) may be blameless in the day of our Lord Jesus Christ" (vv. 7-8). But we can enjoy fellowship with our Lord even while we await His return. Before we know Him by sight, we can walk with Him by faith until the end, when our fellowship with Him reaches its pinnacle.

That fellowship is found particularly through the breaking of the bread and the blessing of the cup, through which we enjoy a participation (*koinonia*) in the body and the blood of Christ (1 Cor. 10:16). Jesus instituted the Lord's Supper so that His followers might remember His death (1 Cor. 11:24-25), but He never meant that we be mere spectators of a drama, content to watch and listen. We are partakers of the supper, so we must eat and drink. In other words, Christ means that we are not only to remember His death, but that we are also to share in its benefits by faith.

Paul explains that when we partake of the Lord's Supper we participate in the body and blood of Christ. It is vital that we understand "the body and blood of Christ" means His death and its consequent benefits. The broken bread stands for the body of Jesus, not as it lived in Palestine, but as it was given in death on the cross. The poured wine stands for the blood of Jesus, not as it flowed in His veins while He lived, but as it was shed in death on the cross. So the body and blood of Christ signify not His life, but His death. At the

Supper to which He invited us we share not in His life and its power, but in His death and its blessings. There He is presented to us as our crucified Savior, who gave His life for our redemption.

Participation in the body and blood of Christ happens only when the physical act of eating bread and drinking wine is accompanied by faith. Just as our bodies receive the bread and wine by eating and drinking, our souls receive the forgiveness of our sins by faith, of which eating and drinking are the perfect physical equivalent. So the bread and wine are only symbols. Our eyes see the symbols, but our faith looks beyond the symbols to the reality for which they stand, and gratefully appropriates anew the precious body and blood of Christ.

Sometimes we speak of the Lord's Supper as Communion (as translated in the King James Version). The word is from the Latin *communis*, "common." In the Lord's Supper, then, Christians participate in common with one another in the salvation benefits that result from the outpoured blood and the broken body of Christ. It is here above all that Christians find fellowship with the Lord and with each other. The Communion service is the chief expression of fellowship between Kingdom citizens. The Church of England catechism describes it as "a sign of the love that Christians ought to have among themselves one to another." Five times in 1 Corinthians 11, in the space of eighteen verses, Paul uses the verb "to come together." The Lord's Supper is a gathering together of Christian people. Many churches observe a beautiful custom during their Communion services. The various communicants share their bread with one another in an act of reciprocal giving and receiving, indicating their oneness. Paul expresses the truth of our oneness in 1 Corinthians 10:17: "For we, though many, are one bread and one body; for we all partake of that one bread." The bread is an emblem of the crucified Savior, and it is our common participation in Him, symbolized by our common participation in it, that makes us one.

Fellowship with God the Holy Spirit

Finally, Christians are granted "the fellowship of the Holy Spirit" (2 Cor. 13:14; Phil. 2:1), who dwells in all the people of God and makes them to be "partakers (*koinonoi*) of the divine nature" (2 Pet. 1:4). Fellowship is inevitable among all those who have been quickened by the Holy Spirit out of spiritual death and given new life in Jesus Christ. Indeed, it is possible only because of our common participation in the Spirit and because the Spirit Himself effects that fellowship. Thus, *koinonia* is something created by the Spirit. It is more than a product of our humanity; it partakes of the supernatural. Try as we may, we can neither create nor duplicate *koinonia*. Because of the spiritual nature of true fellowship, only the activity of the Holy Spirit can bring it into being.

The early Christians never tried to organize fellowship in a semi-professional way, saying, "It's our duty as Christians to be brotherly, so let's have a meeting to promote brotherhood." Such an attempt would have seemed to them utterly trivial and foolish. Their fellowship arose from and found its definition in the fact that they were sharing together the very life of Jesus, communicated to them by the Holy Spirit. Far too often today we have the mistaken notion that we can run a superhuman fellowship on a human basis. It can't be done! We have tried to organize and mechanize and work the thing up, failing to realize that the fellowship of the church is going to be just as limited, just as disruptive, just as much at the mercy of temperament and frail human nature as all the other fellowships of this world—unless it is true to its own supernatural origin and builds on an experience of Christ.

The church is not an organization, something put together by human effort and ingenuity; it is a divine-human organism, a living spiritual entity. A bouquet of flowers might be considered an organization—beautiful if skillfully arranged, but man-made and prone to wither and fall apart. A flowering plant, however, is an organism—alive, integrated, growing.

It's not without significance that the first time the word *koinonia* occurs in the New Testament is in Acts 2:42, where Luke describes the life of the church following Pentecost. But it's no wonder, because there could be no true "fellowship" before the Spirit came at Pentecost, because Christian fellowship is essentially "the fellowship of the Spirit," our common participation in Him. It is His indwelling presence in each of us that makes us the one body of Christ. When He came He bestowed upon the infant church, among other things, the gift of *koinonia*. Here is the only explanation for the early Christian community that Luke describes in Acts. Immediately after the Spirit created the fellowship, "all who believed were together" (2:44). Luke does not mean for us to understand that they actually lived together, and that the first Christian commune was established in Jerusalem. We note in verse 46 that they still lived in private houses. The statement in verse 44 means that they were keenly aware that they belonged together as a family of brothers and sisters who were sharers of God's great gift of the Holy Spirit.

So we have a common relationship with God as our Father, a common experience with Jesus Christ as our Savior, and a common participation in the Holy Spirit as our indwelling comforter. We are begotten by the will and word of the same Father, redeemed by the blood of the same Son, and indwelt by the presence of the same Spirit. Then it is our common share in God as Father, Son, and Holy Spirit that makes us one and constitutes our fellowship. Biblical *koinonia*, therefore, is not just a matter of friendliness, of pleasing personality, or of desiring to do good together. It is something that lifts us up into the realm of the blessed Trinity. We must always think of Christian oneness in this exalted way, and never merely in terms of human cooperation and organization.

Fellowship Necessitates Holiness

The fact that we have come to share in a common salvation by grace through faith does not grant us the license to relax in indolence or sin. Fellowship with the God who is light is morally conditioned, for it is not for those who have chosen to walk in darkness (1 John 1:6). Fellowship with God is an incentive to holiness, and it is actually impossible apart from holiness. Since the Holy Spirit makes us to be "partakers of the divine nature" (2 Pet. 1:4), sin is incongruous in the life of one who claims to have the nature of God. Sin is always a barrier to fellowship with God (see Ps. 5:4; 66:18; Isa. 59:1-2), because "what fellowship has light with darkness?" (2 Cor. 6:14). We might well regard with suspicion those who claim intimate relationship with God, but who live in total disregard to His demands for holiness.

If walking in darkness disrupts one's fellowship with God, walking in the light has the opposite effect. "Blessed are the people who . . . walk, O Lord, in the light of Your countenance" (Ps. 89:15). So in 1 John 1:7 the apostle affirms the result of walking in the light. Since in the previous verse he declared that walking in the darkness prevents fellowship with God, we could now expect him to state the opposite truth that walking in the light leads to fellowship with God. That is certainly true, but instead he declares that walking in the light makes it possible for us to enjoy fellowship with one another. Once again we face the incontrovertible reality of the interdependence of the two fellowships (see v. 3).

Fellowship and Trials

There is yet another aspect of our sharing in a common experience to consider. Contrary to some deceitful teachings, salvation does not exempt us from various kinds of trials. Quite the opposite is true, because fellowship with Christ includes "the fellowship of His sufferings" (Phil. 3:10). The apostle Peter exhorts us not to be surprised at persecution (1 Pet. 4:12), and reminds us that we "partake of Christ's sufferings" (v. 13). John identified himself as our "companion in the tribulation and kingdom and patience of Jesus Christ" (Rev. 1:9). The entire New Testament presents us with the fact that we must expect to suffer if we follow in the train of our King (see Matt. 5:10-12; John 15:18-24; 1 Pet. 4:12-16; Acts 14:22; 2 Tim. 3:12). The references, of course, are to the anti-Christian hostility of the world, which takes the form of rejection, slander and persecution. We should not be surprised if such activity increases, but rather we should be surprised if it does not. We would do well to remember the words of Jesus in Luke 6:26: "Woe to you when all men speak well of you." He indicated that universal popularity was just as much the lot of the false prophets as persecution was of the true ones.

Dietrich Bonhoeffer well understood the inevitability of suffering for the sake of the gospel. He was unwavering in his Christian opposition to the Nazi regime, even though it meant for him imprisonment, torture, and finally execution. Here is what he believed and taught:

> Suffering, then, is the badge of true discipleship. The disciple is not above his master. Following Christ means *passio passiva*, suffering because we have to suffer. That is why Luther reckoned suffering among the marks of the true Church, and one of the memoranda drawn up in preparation for the Augsburg Confession similarly defines the Church as the community of those 'who are persecuted and martyred for the gospel's sake.' . . . Discipleship means allegiance to the suffering Christ, and it is therefore not At all surprising that Christians should be called upon to suffer. In fact, it is a joy and a token of his grace. {Dietrich Bonhoeffer, *The Cost of Discipleship* (London: SCM, 1959), pp. 80, 81.}

However, in the midst of sufferings endured for the sake of Christ, "rejoice to the extent that you partake of Christ's sufferings, that when His glory is revealed you may also be glad with exceeding joy" (1 Pet. 5:1). Why should you rejoice? Peter declares that you will also be "a partaker (*koinonos*) of the glory that will be revealed" (1 Pet. 5:1). It's no wonder that Jesus Himself encouraged us to "rejoice and be exceedingly glad, for great is your reward in heaven" (Matt. 5:12).

Here, then, is the basic meaning of *koinonia*: a common sharing in grace now and in glory hereafter, but also of suffering meanwhile. Christian fellowship is our common participation in God's "great salvation" (Heb. 2:3).

A Co-operative Service

Fellowship is not just a theoretical, or an emotional, or a doctrinal matter; it is intensely practical, expressing not only what we **share in** together, but what we **share out** together. New Testament *koinonia* speaks not only of what we have received together, but of what we give together. We have the experience of common salvation, and we are to "work out" that salvation (Phil. 2:12). Therefore, our common possession necessitates a common service.

Partnership in Evangelism

This aspect of fellowship in the New Testament involves a sharing out of two things. First, we are partners in sharing the gospel. We noted earlier that *koinonia* was commonly used in secular Greek for a business partnership. The same use is found in Luke 5:10, which states that James and John were "partners" with Simon in the fishing business. Immediately after the disciples had successfully landed their tremendous haul of fish, Jesus said to Simon: "Do not be afraid. From now on you will catch men." The church, then, may be regarded as a fellowship of fishermen who are *koinonia*, partners with Jesus and with one another in the great business of catching men. Paul referred to both Titus (2 Cor. 8:23) and Philemon (Phm.17) as his partners (*koinonoi*), and he particularly mentioned how Philemon had shared (*koinonia*) his faith with others (v. 6).

This partnership in the work of the gospel is not confined to a select few, because all Christians are partners in this great activity. This fact is well illustrated in Philippians 1:5, where Paul gave thanks to God for the Philippian Christians' "fellowship in the gospel" that had been constant from the day they had first received the good news. A significant feature of Paul's statement is his use of the Greek preposition *eis*, which means more than "in," as it is translated here. The word indicates that their fellowship in the gospel was not merely a passive enjoyment of all its benefits, but rather it was an active participation in the spread of the gospel.

An interesting use of the word *koinonia* in relation to the furtherance of the gospel is found in Galatians 2:9, where Paul describes how he and Barnabas received from the Jerusalem apostles "the right hand of fellowship." This gesture was far more meaningful than a friendly greeting. It signified a recognition of partnership in world evangelization, with different spheres allocated in which to preach the gospel, "that we should go to the Gentiles and they to the circumcised." In fact, the New English Bible translates, "(They) accepted Barnabas and myself as partners, and shook hands upon it."

Partners in Giving

The second thing that Christian partners share out together is material possessions. Christian responsibility does not end with evangelism, because loving involvement with individuals, once begun, cannot simply be turned off. Christianity is intensely practical, and Christian love makes no analytical distinctions between soul and body. As we have seen, love is more than an emotional feeling. It is vigorously motional, expressing itself in doing. It was so with God Himself: "For God so loved . . . that He gave . . ." (John 3:16).

Jesus is our pattern in this aspect of sharing. His was a compassionate mission, and what aroused His compassion was always human need, in whatever form He encountered it. That compassion he felt for people called forth action. Of course, the climax of His self-giving service was His atoning death, by which He secured our redemption. However, His compassionate mission was not limited to the spiritual realm, because human need also involves the physical realm. Neither should our concern be limited exclusively to evangelism. It is true that humanity's most fundamental need is salvation through the death and resurrection of Christ. Nothing is more liberating, and nothing is more humanizing than being reconciled to God, experiencing a new birth, and having the assurance that sins are forgiven. But this is not earth's only need, and authentic Christian compassion will not allow us to turn a blind eye to human need of any form. There need not be any controversy between evangelism and social action, because needs of body and needs of soul are both valid. Our Lord did not limit His compassion, and neither must we. Christian evangelistic and social activities are both compassionate responses to human need.

Both Old and New Testament teachings make it quite clear that God expects His people to see the needs of one another. Can we say with David, "I have not seen the righteous forsaken nor his descendants begging bread" (Ps. 37:25)? If we can't, we have reason to question whether our church is fulfilling its biblical responsibility of sharing material possessions.

On one occasion I was in a church service where almost 2,000 people were gathered. The pastor asked those with urgent financial needs to stand, upon which about seventy-five people rose to their feet. He then led in a fervent prayer that God would meet their needs and bless them with prosperity. There was no suggestion of any responsibility on the part of brothers and sisters in the congregation to help in any way beyond general intercessory prayer. But is this to be the limit of our personal involvement in doing "good to all, especially to those who are of the household of faith" (Gal. 6:10)?

Love begets love. Because we have received love we are constrained to share that love, which will find expressions in concern and service. Ethel Arnold Tilden has caught this aspect of the function of a real church:

We dedicate a church today.
Lord Christ I pray
Within the sound of its great bell
There is no mother who must hold
Her baby close against the cold--
So only have we served Thee well;
The wind blows sharp, the snow lies deep.
If we shall keep
Thy hungry ones, and sore distressed,
From pain and hardship, then may we
Know we have builded unto Thee,
And that each spire and arch is blest.
Lord Christ, grant we may consecrate
To Thee this church we dedicate.

{"Dedication," *Masterpieces of Religious Verse*, J. D. Morrison, ed. (New York: (Harper and Row, 1948), p. 488.}

There is oftentimes a great deal of unbrotherliness among brothers. Moses saw that unseemly reality when he asked: "Men, you are brethren; why do you wrong one another?" (Acts 7:26). It is a natural thing for Christians to show a mutual affection, not only by avoiding wrongdoing to all, but by seeking the well being of each. The Greek word for "generous" is the same as the word for "fellowship" (*koinonia*). The direct opposite of *koinonia* is the word *pleonexia*, which describes the grasping spirit that is concerned only for itself. In strong contrast to the spirit of selfish getting, therefore, the spirit of generous sharing characterizes Kingdom fellowship. The New Testament presents this idea of the word *koinonia* several times. In 1 Timothy 6:18 Paul exhorts rich people to be "ready to give (*eumetadotoi*, a kindred word to *koinonia*), willing to share (*koinonia*)." All Christians are not to "forget to do good and to share" (*koinonia*), and they are to remember that "with such sacrifices God is well pleased" (Heb. 13:16). We are to be diligent in "distributing (*koinoneo*) to the needs of the saints" (Rom. 12:13). Paul uses the same word three times for the "contribution" of the Macedonian and Achaian churches to the poor saints at Jerusalem (Rom. 15:26; 2 Cor. 8:4; 9:13). He also employed the word to instruct those who are taught to "share" with their teachers (Gal. 6:6; see Phil. 4:15).

The early church provides the best example of this feature of fellowship. We read that after Pentecost "all who believed were together, and had all things in common (*koina*, the same root as *koinonia*), and sold their possessions and goods, and divided them among all, as anyone had need" (Acts 2:44-45). This report does not make it mandatory for every Christian to sell his property and give the money away. Nowhere does the New Testament forbid private property. It's apparent from verse 46 that the believers met in their homes, indicating that some had kept theirs. Furthermore, Peter later told Ananias that his property both before and after its sale was his own, to do with as he pleased (Acts 5:4).

Although the New Testament does not demand that we sell all our possessions or to hold them in common, it does demand that we be good and generous stewards of what we own, and to exercise compassionate care for those in need. Both the Old and the New Testament repeatedly command compassion and generosity as qualities to be maintained. On the basis of such evident biblical teachings, we must conclude that every true follower of King Jesus is sensitive to the needs of others in the Kingdom of God. No one can turn a blind eye or harden his heart to the needs of his brothers and sisters and still claim to be filled with the Holy Spirit. The early church was a caring community, and Christians were guided by two principles that are clearly stated in the book of Acts. They distributed to all "as anyone had need" (2:45; 4:35), and they gave "each according to his ability" (11:29). Those principles are still valid guidelines today. We are to practice Christian generosity by each one giving according to his ability to each one according to his need.

This feature of genuine fellowship is well illustrated in 1 John 3:17-18, which gives the evidence of the indwelling of divine love. First, divine love **sees** the needs of others: "Whoever . . . sees his brother in need . . ." The force of the verb suggests much more than a mere, casual, passing glance that impresses nothing particular on the observer's mind, such as that demonstrated by the "certain priest" in the parable of the Good Samaritan (Luke 10:31). The priest noticed the tremendous need of the victim, but he gave it no second thought. Notice that the priest was "going down" from Jerusalem. If he had been going up, perhaps we could excuse his heartlessness on the grounds that to delay would make him late for his temple duties, or that contact with this apparently dead body would ceremonially disqualify him from those duties. However, that wasn't at all the case, because he had already performed his religious responsibilities. He just didn't care, and therefore he took no heed of desperate need.

It is always characteristic of true love to be observant, to see the needs to which selfishness is blind.

In the second place, divine love **feels** the needs of others: "Whoever . . . sees his brother in need, and shuts up his heart from him . . ." In contrast to the priest and the Levite, who "passed by on the other side" when they saw the helpless victim, the Samaritan "had compassion" when he saw him (Luke 10:33). The statement of 1 John 3:17 assumes that those who have the love of God in them will feel what they see. The sight of need will immediately arouse their godly compassion. Once again, Jesus is our example. Many times He "was moved with compassion"—by leaderless or hungry crowds (Matt. 9:36; 15:32), by the sick and the blind (Matt. 14:14; 20:34), by a single leper (Mark 1:41), by a widow who had lost her only child (Luke 7:13). "Therefore, as the elect of God, holy and beloved," let us "put on tender mercies, kindness . . ." (Col. 3:12).

Finally, divine love **acts** to relieve the needs of others: "Let us not love in word or in tongue, but in deed and in truth." The love that Jesus exemplified is positive, seeking the other person's good, and it leads to activity on behalf of that person, even at personal cost. Can we not follow the King's example? What His eyes saw, His heart felt, and what His heart felt, His hand touched.

In 2 Corinthians 8 Paul referred to an offering to relieve the poverty of the Jerusalem saints. To motivate the Corinthians to generosity, he cited the example of the Macedonian Christians. Although they were experiencing deep poverty themselves, they joyfully gave, not according to their ability but beyond their ability. In fact, their desire to give was so passionate that they begged the apostle that they might share in this fellowship of ministering to the saints. Their plea was not that of affluent Gentiles who wished to minister to their "less fortunate" neighbors, but that of Christians suffering for the sake of other Christians whom they had never even seen, depriving themselves without even the prospect of looking into the grateful eyes of those who received the gift at the moment they received it.

So Christian fellowship is Christian caring, and Christian caring is Christian sharing—not only of our possessions, but also of our time, our sympathy, our service, and ourselves—and that generously. All this active, purposive service arises from the fundamental fact that we belong to one another. We are our brother's keeper precisely because we are brothers. Those early Christians loved one another, and they expressed their love in sacrificial service. That kind of relationship is not surprising, since the first fruit of the Spirit is love (Gal. 5:22). You can give without loving, but you cannot love without giving.

A Reciprocal Responsibility

The third facet of *koinonia* involves what we **share with** one another. If we were to picture the different aspects of fellowship, we would see ourselves facing certain directions. When we portray what we share in our experience together, we are all facing the Lord who gave Himself for us. When we visualize what we share out together, our co-operative service, we are all facing other people whom we are seeking to serve. But when we depict what we share with one another, we are not all facing the same direction. Instead, we are gathered in a circle, facing each other. In the first fellowship, we are all recipients; in the second, we are all givers; but in the third, we are all involved in what Paul calls a "partnership . . . concerning giving and receiving" (Phil. 4:15).

This aspect of fellowship was characteristic of the Christian community immediately after Pentecost. We have already noted that they "had all things in common" (Acts 2:44), meaning that they shared their material possessions with each other. It was a kind of reciprocal aid arrangement wherein they engaged in a fellowship of giving and receiving.

However, this mutual sharing was not restricted to money. As an example, the partnership of giving and receiving of which Paul spoke in Philippians 4:15 was a matter of his giving the gospel to them and their sending a gift to him. A similar sharing is found in 1 Corinthians 9:11, where Paul asked, "If we have sown spiritual things for you, is it a great thing if we reap your material things?" Similarly, he exhorted the Galatians to "let him who is taught the word share in all good things with him who teaches" (Gal. 6:6).

On his third missionary journey, Paul took a collection among the Greek churches for the relief of the poor saints in Jerusalem. In the primary sense, the collection was a voluntary offering, but Paul also regarded it as the repayment of a debt for something the Gentiles had received from the Jews. It was a token of the mutual responsibility of the Jews and the Gentiles, "for if the Gentiles have been partakers of their (the Jews) spiritual things, their duty is also to minister to them in material things" (Rom. 15:26-27).

The New Testament strongly emphasizes the interdependence of Christians, and the many exhortations dealing with proper attitudes and conduct toward one another all grow out of an awareness of this mutual responsibility. Paul was an authoritative apostle and he enjoyed spiritual experiences that few people have known; yet he was humble enough to admit his need of help from others. He may have been a spiritual superstar, but he was not above the need of intercessory prayer, so he earnestly desired the prayers of Christians everywhere (Rom. 15:30; Col. 4:3; 1 Thess. 5:25; 2 Thess 3:1; see 2 Cor. 1:11; Phil. 1:19; Phm. 22). Despite his close relationship with Christ, his communion with the Holy Spirit and visitations with angels, he still confessed his need for human friendship (2 Cor. 7:6; 2 Tim. 4:9, 11, 21). Romans 1:11-12 provides a clear example of

Paul's awareness of mutual dependence among kingdom citizens. There he states his ardent desire to visit the Romans that he might strengthen them by imparting some spiritual gift to them, and also that he would receive encouragement together with them by their mutual faith.

Only a full awareness that we need each other, and an acceptance of the mutual responsibilities arising from that awareness, strengthens our fellowship. Kingdom citizens are not to live in isolation, guarding their own privacy as a sacred treasure, and thinking to insure their own safety by refusing to allow themselves to become involved in the affairs of other citizens. A keep-your-distance impersonal approach to brotherhood does not bring safety and maturity, but they are found in a big-brotherliness that is just as much concerned with the needs of others in the Kingdom as with your own. The entire life of Jesus was one of giving, but He received as rightfully due Him the homage and worship of those whom He served. When individual Christians humble themselves both to give and receive from one another, facing each other in a circle on interdependency, the witness of the church to the world will be irresistible.

Here, then, is the threefold aspect of *koinonia* that the New Testament teaches. We share in a common experience together; we share out together in co-operative service; and we share with one another in a reciprocal responsibility. In the first aspect of fellowship we receive together, in the second we give together, while in the third we engage in mutual giving and receiving.

IV

ONE-ANOTHERNESS: NEGATIVES

Citizens of the Kingdom of God are of different cultures, races, nationalities, and social strata, and they may wear different denominational labels. Despite all these earthly distinctions, in Christ we are one, "fellow citizens with the saints and members of the household of God" (Eph. 2:15, 19).

No Cliqueism in God's Kingdom

Just before the meeting began at a Methodist church where I was speaking at a Christian life conference, I was sitting on the platform next to the pastor. He called my attention to a distinguished looking man who had just entered the auditorium, identifying him as the pastor of a Baptist church just down the street. He concluded his identification with the remark, "He's our competition."

I knew, of course, what he meant, but I looked at him in mock astonishment. "Just a moment," I said. "This man is the pastor of the Baptist church just down the street?"

"That's right," he confirmed.

"And he's working for the devil?"

"I didn't say that!" he protested.

"But you said he was your competition!"

This gentle rebuke was forceful enough to drive home the point that I wanted to make, which is that Christian churches and individual Christians are not in competition with one another. It is indeed true that we are running a race, but that race is not being run against each other. The oneness of the body of Christ precludes any sense of rivalry. That fact is true of individual Christians, of churches, and of denominations. If the Lord is blessing you and your ministry mightily, then I'm to praise Him for doing it and rejoice with you. If the local Baptist church is having a tremendous revival, with souls being saved and lives changed, then the Methodists and the Presbyterians and all other Christians in town ought to give thanks to God.

On one occasion when I was in a large mid-western city, I visited a prominent church of a certain denomination. Placed in conspicuous spots throughout the building were posters announcing a rally to be held at the downtown Civic Center. The same proclamation was included as a bulletin insert. The notice described the meeting as a gigantic display of the strength of that denomination in the city. It went so far as to encourage the people of that persuasion to attend "so we can show this city who we are," naming the denomination. There was not a word about honoring Christ. There was no invitation to all Christians of the city to come together in a demonstration of oneness in common praise of the Lord. The attitude was simply, "Let's show the people of this city who **we** are."

That kind of exclusiveness has no place in the Kingdom of God. Nowadays in our denominational assemblies, we hear about the Lutherans this, the Episcopalians that, the Baptists this, that and the other, etc. There is nothing wrong with denominational groupings, and denominational references may be necessary, but we can become so denominationally self-conscious and voluminously self-advertising that we effectively obscure the vision of Christ. As the fire of the Holy Spirit individually warms us, the result will inevitably be a thawing out in Christian relationships. If we are to win the world according to John 17, all of the King's subjects must live in contagious fellowship.

We cannot escape the fact that, being bound to Christ the King, we are thereby bound to one another. Like the spokes of a wheel, being so close to the axle, we are near to one another. It was the joy and strength of the relationship between the early believers that so impressed the onlookers in the hostile world in which they lived. We would do well today to pray that, in place of the bickering and backbiting that occasionally disfigure our Christian behavior and stultify our Christian testimony, the church at large might receive a new baptism of love, as in the first days of power. Such a practical evidence of the reality and joy of our fellowship would still impress the world.

We Relate to the King As We Relate to One Another

Scripture makes it clear that God considers the fellowship vital to His purpose and plan for us, and He constantly warns us against doing any harm to it. It is very dangerous for a Christian to fail in practicing love towards a fellow believer, acting or speaking in an unloving way. When we act unseemly towards a brother, it is not only the victim that we injure, but the Lord Himself, who died for us both. Do you realize that you actually treat Christ the same way that you treat a Christian brother or sister? On the Damascus Road, as recorded in Acts 9:4, the risen Lord did not ask. "Saul, why are you persecuting My people?" He asked, "Why are you persecuting Me?" Saul had no intention of persecuting Jesus. As far as he was concerned, Jesus was a dead and buried charlatan. But followers of Christ are the body of Christ, and in persecuting them, Saul was guilty of persecuting Christ Himself.

Jesus gave a vivid description of the final judgment in Matthew 25:31-46. He said that all nations will be gathered together before Him, and He will separate them as the shepherd separates the sheep from the goats. The righteous will be invited to enter into the Father's Kingdom, while the unrighteous will be consigned to eternal punishment. Service rendered or not rendered to the Lord will be the hinge on which judgment shall turn. The righteous fed the hungry Lord, gave drink to a thirsty Lord, showed hospitality to a weary Lord, clothed a naked Lord, ministered to a sick Lord and visited an imprisoned Lord. The unrighteous did none of those deeds. However, the reaction of each group will be the same: "Lord, when did we see You in those situations and ministered (or did not minister) to You?" Hear the Lord's response: "Inasmuch as you did (or did not do) it unto the least of these My brethren, you did (or did not do) it unto me."

Would it make any difference in your relationship to your brothers and sisters if you really believed that you were treating Christ the same way? To anyone who harasses a Christian, the Lord says, "Why are you persecuting Me?" To anyone who performs a deed of love to a child of God, the Lord says, "You are doing it to Me." To anyone who "has this world's goods, and sees his brother in need, and shuts up his heart from him" (1 John 3:17), the Lord says, "You refused to help Me."

Before St. Francis dedicated his life to God, he was a vain man, loving finery and abhorring the unattractive. One day while riding, he came upon a loathsome leper, whose features were disfigured and whose robes were filthy with the seepage from his cankers. Strangely moved with pity, St. Francis dismounted his splendid horse and embraced the filthy leper. Suddenly, in the mind of St. Francis came a vision in which the leper was changed into the form of Christ. As he loved "the least of these My brethren," so he loved Christ! A kindness done to a brother is a kindness done to the Lord, but remember that a kindness withheld from a brother is a kindness withheld from the Lord.

In Ephesians 4:32 Paul exhorted, "Be kind to one another, tenderhearted, forgiving one another." He based his appeal on the fact that "God in Christ forgave you." In the very next verse, 5:1, he made another appeal based on God's gracious attitude and generous actions towards us: "Therefore be imitators of God as dear children." Just as children imitate their parents, so we are to copy our Father God. We are also to follow Christ "and walk in love, as Christ also has loved us and given Himself for us, an offering and a sacrifice to God for a sweet-smelling aroma" (v. 2). The inferences are unmistakably clear. If we imitate our Father, we will deal with one another in positive kindness and we will not withhold our forgiveness. If we follow Christ we will give ourselves up to self-sacrificial love, realizing that such self-giving is a sacrifice acceptable to God.

The Key to Kingdom Relationships

The key to living by the pattern set before us in Ephesians 5:32–6:2, and indeed the key to all true Kingdom fellowship, is found in the biblical instructions concerning what I call "one-anotherness." The most common use of *allelous*, "one another," is of reciprocal love. We have already noted the repeated command of Jesus that we love one another as He has loved us. The same command is echoed by the apostles in the following verses: Romans 12:10; 13:8; 1 Thessalonians 3:12; 4:9; 1 Peter 1:22; 1 John 3:11, 23; 4:7, 11-12; 2 John 5. All the remaining verses in the New Testament that deal with one-anotherness are the outworking, both negative and positive of this mutual love. The negative aspect of love is an attitude of **restraint**, while the positive is an attitude of **constraint**. Love, then is both **holding back** and **letting go**. Both of these qualities are attributed to God in Romans 2:4, which speaks of His "goodness" and "longsuffering." Let's examine first some "don'ts" that we are to avoid in reciprocal fellowship.

The Greatest Threat to Kingdom Relationships

The writers of the New Testament were realists enough not to anticipate that the Kingdom community on earth would be perfect. On the contrary, they assumed that problems in relationships would arise, causing tensions in the fellowship. All of the "don'ts" in Kingdom relationships spring from false, arrogant opinions that individuals entertain concerning themselves. For example, in Galatians 5:26, Paul exhorted, "Let us not become conceited, provoking one another, envying one another." This command indicates that our opinion of ourselves determines our attitude and conduct towards others. It is when we are self-conceited, exaggerating our own importance, that we react negatively towards our brothers and sister. The word translated "conceited" describes someone who has an empty, vain notion about himself, maintaining an illusion about himself. To put it bluntly, he is a self-centered egotist. It is absolutely impossible for a person to have that kind of puffed-up attitude about himself and at the same time have the proper attitude towards others, because conceit poisons relationships with other people. In fact, whenever relationships with other people deteriorate, pride is nearly always the basic cause.

According to Galatians 5:26, when we are conceited we tend to react in one of two ways—we either "provoke" one another or "envy" one another. This verse is the only time the New Testament uses the word translated "provoke." The word literally means "to call forth," in the sense of challenging someone to a contest. The implication of the word in this context is that you are so certain of your superiority that you want to demonstrate it. Therefore, you challenge people to dispute your supremacy so you might have an opportunity to prove it.

The word for "envy" describes one of the most warped and twisted of human emotions. It is a quality that springs from an embittered mind that begrudges the fact that another person has certain characteristics or possessions at all. For example, here is a person who is gentle and wise, who is much sought after as a speaker or counselor, and in whose ministry the gifts of the Spirit are mightily operative. The envy of Galatians 5:26 does not necessarily describe an attitude that desires what that person has; it describes the attitude that is bitter because the other person has those things at all. It does not so much want the thing for itself; it merely wants to take them from the other person. The Stoics defined it as "grief at someone else's good." This attitude is worse than jealousy, because it is bitterness that another person is blessed.

Envy is one of the deadliest poisons. It blights and cramps our lives and distorts our judgment. Nothing the other person can do is right. We hate the sound of his voice; we loathe his expressions; while underneath it all, we fume with envy. We run down before others those whom we envy. We would rather see people not converted or healed than to have them blessed through the ministry of the one whom we envy. Every time a committee is appointed Satan immediately starts to work on those who think they should have been on it. Every time a brother receives recognition, the devil plants critical thoughts, provoking people to envy.

What Paul has written here is true to human experience. Generally speaking, when we have an inflated view of self, we are motivated by feelings either of inferiority of superiority. If we feel that we are superior to others, we challenge them, because we want them to acknowledge our superiority. On the other hand, if we feel that they are superior to us, we react in jealousy and envy. In either case our attitude may be attributed to the "conceit" that Paul described—the fantasized opinion of ourselves that will not bear rivals. It's a sad truth that "where envy and self-seeking exist, confusion and every evil thing are there" (James 3:16).

The Power of the Holy Spirit

Directly opposite from these attitudes is the love that is the fruit of the Holy Spirit, which Christians exhibit when they are walking in the Spirit. Rather than manifesting qualities of self-conceited people, those who are controlled by the Spirit follow the dictates that Paul gave in Romans 12:3—they don't think of themselves more highly than they ought to think; they think soberly. When the Holy Spirit opens our eyes in the matter of mutual relationships, He does two things for us. First, He shows us our own unworthiness apart from the grace of God, for without that grace we are really nothing but undeserving, hell-deserving sinners. Then the Spirit convinces us of the worth and importance of other people in the sight of God. Certainly it will take the love that is the product of the Holy Spirit to carry out the exhortation of Philippians 2:3: "Let nothing be done through selfish ambition or conceit, but in lowliness of mind let each esteem others better than himself."

Service, not a sense of competition, should always govern Kingdom relationships. The correct attitude to our brothers and sisters in the Lord is not, "I'm superior to you and I'll prove it." Neither is it, "You're superior to me and I resent it." The only proper attitude is, "You are my brother or my sister, infinitely precious in the sight of God, and it's my joy and privilege to serve you."

The Evil of Malicious Speech

Because these sins of attitude find expression in speech, the New Testament tells us that we are not to "judge" one another (Rom. 14:13), "bite and devour" one another (Gal. 5:15), "lie" to one another (Col. 3:9), "speak evil against" one another (James 4:11), "grumble against" one another (James 5:9). A coal of resentment, bitterness, or jealousy left to smolder in the heart will soon burst forth in fiery words of accusation, criticism and slander. Truly, "the tongue is a fire" (James 3:6), and it has ruined many more lives than bullets or poison. The word that James uses for "speak evil of" (4:11) usually means to speak evil of someone else in that person's absence, when he is not there to defend himself. Throughout its entirety, the

Bible condemns this sin of slander, insult, and evil speaking against a brother. The Psalmist accuses the wicked man: "You sit and speak against your brother; you slander your own mother's son" (Psa. 50:20). God has declared, "Whoever secretly slanders his neighbor, him I will destroy" (Psa. 101:5).

Paul lists slander (the same word of James 4:11, sometimes translated "backbiting") among the sins that characterize the pagan world (Rom. 1:30), and it is one of the sins that he fears he will find in the factious church at Corinth (2 Cor. 12:20). It is not without significance that in both of those passages the word is used in immediate connection with "whisperings," translated in some versions as "gossip." Slander, or backbiting, is the sinful product of those who gather together in little groups and share juicy tidbits of whispered information that destroy the reputation of people who are not there to defend themselves. Peter strongly condemns this sin and characterizes it as a mark of spiritual immaturity (1 Pet. 2:1). In fact, there are few sins that the Bible so unsparingly condemns as the sin of irresponsible and malicious gossip. That condemnation is not without good reason, for failure to discipline "the unruly member" of the body (the tongue, James 3:8) has caused terrible havoc in human relationships. The evils caused by gossip, destructive criticism and idle words enable us to understand our Lord's severe statement: "For every idle word men may speak, they will give account of it in the day of judgment. For by your words you will be justified and by your words you will be condemned" (Matt. 12:36, 37).

Yet, there are few activities that delight the average person more than spicy gossip. To tell and to listen to some slanderous story is a fascinating activity. Most always, the source of the story, and hence the authority for its truthfulness is "they." The most dangerous phrase in the English language is "they say," but nobody apparently has ever been able to identify "they." If only we could locate "they" in order to put a stop to their polluting activity, relationships in society in general would be sweetened in a moment and half the ills of the church would immediately be healed.

Recently someone passed on to me a particularly devastating piece of news about a Christian brother who was well known in the community where he lived. My reaction was quite unexpected by the person who gave the report. "I've got to go to him at once," was my response.

"Why?" my informant asked in astonishment.

My answer was pointed and, I think, biblical: "If it's true, I've got to minister to him (see Gal. 6:1); if it isn't true, then we've got to put a stop to such a vicious rumor."

Taming the Tongue

Taming the tongue is a most important aspect of Christian discipline all too lightly ignored by many Kingdom citizens. Several questions concerning our utterances may be helpful in establishing this discipline, and of co-operating with God in answering the prayer: "Set a guard, O Lord, over my mouth; keep watch over the door of my lips" (Psa. 141:3).

Is it true? A Christian should never, of course, say anything that is not true; yet we often give false impressions by exaggeration, by distortion, by withholding all the facts, by half quoting and other departures from strict honesty of word. For example, a leading Christian journal, generally regarded as the voice of America's evangelical community, recently included a report on one of the foremost charismatic ministries in the United States. The article was grossly misleading, not so much because of what it said, but because of what it did not say, leaving the reader with a distorted picture of that ministry. Accuracy in speech is more difficult than is commonly supposed, but it can be attained with practice. In this respect we need especially to be on guard when speaking of those we do not naturally "like."

Is it kind? One of the greatest evils of the tongue is the negative and destructive criticism of others in their absence. This practice can be eliminated altogether by observing a simple rule such as the following: "I will not say in anyone's absence that which I would be unwilling to say in his presence." There is a place for constructive criticism, but that should always be made privately to the person concerned, and not to others in his absence.

Is it necessary? Words are precious things, and the Bible repeatedly warns us about the dangers of too much speech. Mr. Talkative is not among the King's pilgrims on the way to the celestial city. I certainly do not decry the mentioning of certain things as a matter of prayerful concern to others, to enlist their aid in intercession, but it is probably true to say that most of us talk far too much, and listen too little. Paul superbly summed up all these suggestions in the great phrase "speaking the truth in love" (Eph. 4:15). If this guideline were followed, much unkind gossip would be avoided, more serious backsliding would be prevented, the good of the church would be advanced, and the name of Christ would be glorified.

The Gravity of Judging Others

The Bible condemns sins of speech against our brothers and sisters for two basic reasons. First, speaking evil against one another is a breach of a fundamental law of the Kingdom, called the royal law in James 2:8 (see James 4:11). The royal law is that we should love our neighbor as ourselves. Jesus, of course, gave greater depth to this law when He taught that we are to love one another as He has loved us. Now, it should be obvious that a person cannot love another as himself or as Christ loves us while at the same time spreading slanderous talk about him. Furthermore, if a person breaks that commandment, knowing that he is disregarding it, he is setting himself above the law of Christ. Or, as James teaches he has made himself a judge of the law, and his judgment is that his own will is more binding than the plain command of the Lord. Therefore, the person who engages in malicious backbiting is guilty of a grievous sin, because he has appointed himself a judge of Christ's teachings, and he has assumed the right to break the commandment of the Lord.

Second, to speak evil of a brother or sister by criticizing, slandering and insulting him is to infringe upon the prerogative of God. It is, in fact, to set yourself up as the judge of your brother or sister, but the right of judgment belongs to God and to God alone. With this teaching of James 4:11, 12, the rest of Scripture concurs (see Matt. 7:1; Rom. 14:4, 13). The prohibition of judging one another is not meant to abolish law courts or to forbid constructive criticism, but to exclude censoriousness. That condemning attitude is a compound sin consisting of several ugly and unpleasant ingredients. Basically, it is to judge people harshly from a haughty attitude of superiority. The censorious critic is a condemning faultfinder who is always negative and destructive towards other people and who actually enjoys pointing out their shortcomings. He always questions their motives, depreciates their plans, and is uncharitable towards their mistakes. Few critics who gleefully expose the faults of others would admit it, but their motive in doing so is to enhance their own standing in the judgment both of God and men. Many people have the mistaken notion that they can lift themselves up by putting others down. That kind of censorious spirit is a pharisaic evil. Exalting oneself by disparaging others is a very cheap way of attaining moral superiority. Jesus gave a commentary on such practices in the parable of the Pharisee and the publican, and "He spoke this parable to some who trusted in themselves that they were righteous and despised others" (Luke 18:9).

Moffatt translates 1 Corinthians 13:6: "Love is never glad when others go wrong: love is gladdened by goodness." That which causes a person to rejoice is a fair test of that person's character. To be glad when evil prevails, or to rejoice in the misdeeds of others, is indicative of great moral degradation.

To judge another, then, is to claim to possess the competence and authority that rightfully only God has. Paul asked, "Who are you to judge another's servant? To his own master he stands or falls" (Rom. 14:4). Paul applied this truth to himself when hostile detractors criticized him: "He who judges me is the Lord. Therefore judge nothing before the time, until the Lord comes, who will both bring to light the hidden things of darkness and reveal the counsels of the hearts" (1 Cor. 4:4-5). The thing that Paul is emphasizing in these verses is the simple but vital truth that an individual cannot presume to be God. No human being is qualified to be the judge of his fellows, for we cannot know each other's hearts or determine each other's motives. To assume the place of a censorious judge is arrogantly to anticipate the day of judgment and to infringe upon the rights of God. It is, in fact, an attempt to play God.

All of these "don'ts" are favorite means of the devil in sowing seeds of discord among the brethren. But at the root of all of them is an unbiblical "puffed-up-ness" that gives birth to various sins of attitude that blind our judgment and spoil our relationships. A once proud Pharisee, graduate of Tarsus, Hebrew of Hebrews, Roman citizen, who might well have gloried in all this, listed the qualities of true *agape* in 1 Corinthians 13. Among its many virtues, love "is not puffed up" (v. 4). Let us learn from the changed attitude of Paul, who instead of assuming a place of lofty superiority over all others, was happy to call the worthless runaway slave Onesimus "a beloved brother, especially to me" (Phm. 16).

V

ONE-ANOTHERNESS: POSITIVES

In tracing the "one another" phrases through the New testament, one must be struck by the fact that there is far more emphasis on the positive outworking of love than on the negative. This feature is in harmony with biblical teachings concerning righteousness. After all, if goodness is only negative, then it's very possible for one to be good, but good for nothing! We are not only to flee immorality (1 Cor. 6:18), idolatry (1 Cor. 10:14), greed (1 Tim. 6:11), youthful lusts (2 Tim. 2:22), and to abstain from the very appearance of evil (1 Thess. 5:22), but we are to pursue righteousness, godliness, faith, love, perseverance, gentleness and peace (1 Tim. 6:11; 2 Tim 2:22; 1 Cor. 14:1; Heb. 12:14; 3 John 11). Especially when it concerns relationships within the Christian community, we are to "pursue the things which make for peace and the things by which one may edify another" (Rom. 14:19), and "always pursue what is good both for yourselves and for all" (1 Thess. 5:15; see Gal. 6:10).

The Basic Precept

Jesus made clear the positive nature of one-anotherness in the giving of the so-called Golden Rule (Matt. 7:12). Many critics assert that the Golden Rule is found in a similar form elsewhere, but they invariably fail to mention that it is always stated negatively elsewhere. For example, Confucius is credited with having said, "Do not to others what you would not wish done to yourself." An almost identical saying is found among the Greek philosophers known as the Stoics. There is a maxim in the Apocrypha that reads, "Do not do to anyone what you yourself would hate" (Tobit 4:15). About the year 20 B.C. a would-be proselyte asked Rabbi Hillel to teach him the whole law while standing on one leg. Hillel, with apparent reference to the verse just quoted, responded: "What is hateful to you, do not do to anyone else. This is the whole law; all the rest is only commentary."

There is a tremendous difference between the negative and rather grudging precept of Hillel ("Don't do to others what is hateful to you" and the positive initiative that Jesus taught ("Do to others what you wish they would do to you"). The principle that our King laid down has such wide application that He could add, "For this is the law and the prophets." In other words, whoever conducts himself towards others in the same manner that he would like others to conduct themselves toward him has fulfilled the law and the prophets, at least in the matter of love for his neighbor (see Rom. 13:8-10).

An awareness of the positive nature of love for one another, especially as stated in the Golden Rule, will transform our actions. If we put ourselves sensitively into the place of our brother, and wish for him what we would wish for ourselves, we would not display the "don'ts" of one-anotherness discussed in the last chapter. We would never be cruel, but always kind; never harsh and bitter in judgment, but always understanding; never selfish, but always generous. Once we are gripped by the fact that we are truly brothers and sisters in the Lord, it is inconceivable that we shall be anything other than caring and constructive in our attitudes towards one another.

Prefer One Another

We have stressed the fact that love is the foundation of true fellowship, and that one-anotherness is an outworking of the love that we are to have for each other. Nowhere is that principle more clearly stated than in Romans 12:10: “Be kindly affectionate to one another with brotherly love, in honor giving preference to one another.” Two significant features stand out in that directive. First, the word for “kindly affectionate” is the Greek word *philostorgos*, used only here in the New Testament. The word denotes very strong **family** love. We must love one another, then, because we are members of one family. The Christian church is not a congregation of mere acquaintances or even a gathering of friends. Such gatherings tend to be aggregations rather than congregations—aggregations of unrelated persons. We are not strangers within the church, isolated in a pew or hiding behind a pillar, holding ourselves aloof from a more intimate Christian fellowship. Anything that encourages the lone-sheep approach, allowing a person to become an outwardly conforming member only by his church attendance, stunts or damages his spiritual progress. The word that Paul chose in Romans 12:10 emphasizes the fact that we are a family.

The second outstanding feature of the verse is the teaching that we are to be self-forgetful in placing others before ourselves. Obedience to this command is particularly difficult, because it strikes at the basic human drive for self-assertion and love of prominence. I firmly believe that the trouble that arises in churches has its origin right at this point. Egoism is the supreme enemy of true fellowship. We are strongly concerned about our own rights and privileges and places and prestige. I thought that I should have been included in that committee. At least they could have consulted me! And why was that person given a more prominent place on the platform that I was? Nobody has even called attention to the hard work that I did!

Can you see how a prideful desire for prominence leads to other sins? It leads to anger because our demands have not been met, to self-pity because our pride is hurt, to a foolish refusal to give in because our ideas were not accepted. So we go on hurting and being hurt because we fail to recognize that love "does not seek its own" (1 Cor. 13:5). The fellowship of saints will always be blighted as long as we entertain the desire for personal prestige, to receive the plaudits of others, to be recognized, to be flattered, to have our opinions sought, to have a platform seat.

Love is not arrogant, but humble (1 Cor. 13:4). Love knows nothing of presumptuous self-satisfaction, of pride with contempt of others (and the two invariably go together), and inflated vanity. It doesn't put on airs and it is never haughty; but it's humble and gracious. The greatest people have always been humble, giving priority to others in honor.

In the last half of the nineteenth century, one of the most widely respected scholars in Great Britain was Dr. John Cairns, a Scottish theologian. When he was a young man he was offered the prestigious position of principal of Edinburgh University, but he declined, preferring to serve his church in a more humble way. Dr. Cairns was also noted for his sincere humility. On public occasions, he customarily stood back and let others pass him, saying, "You first, I follow." On one such occasion he was a member of the platform party at a great gathering. As he approached, there was a tremendous burst of applause. Cairns stood back and let the next man pass, and he joined in the applause. In actuality, he was the one receiving the recognition, but he never imagined that the applause was for him, assuming that it was meant for someone else. When he was dying he said farewell to those whom he loved, but his lips continued to move. Those around him bent to catch his final words, which doubtless were spoken to his Lord, who was dearer to him than life—"You first, I follow." Such lowliness is one of the richest ingredients of love, and in its presence pride becomes impertinence and an offense. Here is an example of putting into practice Peter's exhortation to "be submissive to one another, and be clothed with humility" (1 Pet. 5:5).

The Example of Jesus Christ

Paul repeats the exhortation of Romans 12:10 in Philippians 2:3-4: "Let nothing be done through selfish ambition or conceit, but in lowliness of mind let each esteem others better than himself. Let each of you look out not only for his own interests, but also for the interests of others." What makes this charge especially forceful is that Paul underscores it with the example of Jesus Christ, and in verse 5 he calls upon us to have the same attitude that the Lord displayed when He renounced His own rights for our sakes. Jesus did not rigidly and selfishly insist on clinging to the privileges that were rightfully His in His pre-incarnate state of glory, but "though He was rich, yet for your sakes He became poor, that you through His poverty might become rich" (2 Cor. 8:9). The person who loves with the love of the Lord will not grasp at his own rights, nor view the usefulness of all things only in his own pleasure and advancement, disregardful of the good and pleasure of others. A "me first" attitude that promotes self at the expense of others has no place in the Kingdom of God.

When we consider our Lord's humility, "taking the form of a bondservant, and coming in the likeness of men" (Phil. 2:5-8), and girding Himself with a towel to wash the disciples' feet (John 13), then we should see our own great sinfulness in insisting on our rights instead of concentrating on the rights of others and our duty in serving them. Let us not expect others to minister to us, to cater to our pride and to pander to our desires, but let us remember that "the Son of Man did not come to be served, but to serve, and to give His life a ransom for many" (Mark 10:45), and "a servant is not greater than his master" (John 13:16).

A young family moved into a lovely house in an affluent suburb of a major city. Their house adjoined the property of two widowed sisters who were devoted Christians. The young couple was aloof and arrogant, and they proved to be most non-neighborly. As the months passed, the two widows hardly saw the new residents, who kept very much to themselves and their circle of friends and rebuffed every attempt of the sisters to befriend them. A crisis came when the non-neighborly neighbors sent a message through their housekeeper informing the ladies that their hymn singing and the barking of their watchdog were most annoying.

The natural reaction would have been to rise up and defend one's rights. Some people would have even doubled their noise level, built spite fences, and conducted neighborhood warfare in defense of their wounded ego. On this occasion, however, the two Christians met the crisis by replying with a letter that demonstrated long-suffering restraint.

"Dear Neighbors," the letter read. "We are sorry that our dog has annoyed you, but we live here alone, and we have found it necessary to keep a dog, since prowlers have recently been seen around our property. When your dog barks, we're glad that you have a good watchdog that is protecting you. Whey your little girl cries, and it sounds as if it's right outside our windows, we realize that every normal child cries, and we're glad that you are blessed with a precious little child. When we are wakened early in the morning by the water running into your pool, we're glad that you are able to have such lovely times in that pool. When we hear your beautiful music, we're glad that you have such a medium of self-expression. When your guests' cars start under our bedroom windows at all hours of the night, we're glad that you have so many friends and can enjoy their company. When your tennis balls fly onto our lawn, we will continue to toss them back onto your court, as we have been doing. But please don't ask us to stop our singing. We have had a sorrow in this home deeper than most people could realize, but God's grace has sustained us, and we must express praise and worship."

In answering as they did, the dear ladies were reflecting the attitude of Christ, and the incident became praise to Him and shame to those who were not likeminded.

Build One Another Up

True love for one another will also express itself positively in a desire to build one another up (Rom. 14:19; see 1 Thess. 5:11). Such expression will take several forms. First, we will "receive one another, just as Christ also received us" (Rom. 15:7). We recognize the fact that whoever is in Christ is a new creation (2 Cor. 5:17). A new set of standards is part of this newness of life, so that we no longer judge things or people by the same standards that the world uses. In God's Kingdom, "we regard no one according to the flesh" (2 Cor. 5:16); that is, according to a superficial view. We don't go by outward appearances, but by an inward reality.

I recently read a gripping story that beautifully illustrates this principle. A young soldier, who suffered war injuries in Iraq that left him blind, underwent rehabilitation at Walter Reed Army Hospital. During the course of his convalescence, he and one of the nurses who cared for him fell in love and later married. He had a tremendous devotion to her and loved her dearly. One day he overheard some guests in his home talking about him and his wife. "It was good for her that he was blind, because otherwise he never would have married so homely a woman."

He walked into the room and responded, "I overheard what you said, and I thank God from the depths of my heart for blindness of eyes that might have kept me from seeing the marvelous worth of the soul of the woman who became my wife. She is the most noble character I have ever known, and if the outward appearance of her features is such that it might have masked her inward beauty to my soul, then I am the one who gained by having lost my sight." In our acceptance of one another, let us always remember that God is more concerned with the heart than with the outward appearance (1 Sam. 16:7), and that He prefers holiness to glamour (1 Pet. 3:4).

Loving Correction

Having accepted one another, we foster one another's spiritual growth by seeking "to admonish one another" (Rom. 15:14; Col. 3:16), by being careful to "consider one another in order to stir up love and good works" (Heb. 10:24), and by "exhorting one another," especially in light of the nearness of the Lord's return (Heb. 10:25). It's far easier to give way to the leanings of the old nature to advance our own cause, but the constraint of Christian love causes us to put the interests of others above our own. Therefore, we will not hesitate to warn or rebuke when it is necessary, nor will we fail to take advantage of every opportunity to spur on our fellow citizens in their pilgrimage through this life. Eliphaz unwillingly paid Job a great tribute: "Surely you have instructed many, and you have strengthened weak hands. Your words have upheld him who was stumbling" (Job 4:3, 4). Ideally, "everyone helps his neighbor, and says to his brother, 'Be of good courage!'" (Isa. 41:6).

The instruction of Paul in Galatians 6:1 leaves no doubt that we are to be vitally concerned about the spiritual welfare of other Christians: "Brethren, if a man is overtaken in any trespass, you who are spiritual restore such a one in a spirit of gentleness, considering yourself lest you also be tempted." Here the apostle tells us what to do in the case of a person who falls out of step when walking with the Holy Spirit. Unfortunately, many of us react in ways totally different from Paul's directive. Some people stand by and do nothing, on the pretext that it's none of their business and they don't want to become involved, but the instruction of this verse will not allow such an attitude. On the contrary, here is a clear answer to Cain's irresponsible question, "Am I my brother's keeper?" (Gen. 4:9).

Others, at least figuratively, beat the erring brother over the head with the Bible, despising or condemning him from a lofty attitude of spiritual superiority. If I were perfect, then perhaps I could condemn my brother for his sin, but at that point I would cease to be perfect, wouldn't I?

A lot of people react with indifference to the sin of their brother, shrugging their shoulders at his consequent sufferings with the judgmental comment, "Serves him right," or "Let him stew in his own juice." Suppose you are walking across a dark room with bare feet and you stub your big toe against a piece of furniture. Your toe is throbbing with severe pain. Your hand doesn't reprimand your toe by saying, "Serves you right, Clumsy. You should have looked where you were going. Learn a lesson and be more careful next time." On the contrary, your hand flies to your toe in full sympathy. It soothes your toe, caresses it, and does all it can to bring relief. Why? Because that toe is a member of your body, and every other member of your body is deeply concerned when there is an injury to the toe. That erring brother is a member of the body of Christ, and what affects him affects the entire body.

The world has a perception of the church that, sad to say, we often give cause to justify. Outsiders view the church largely as judgmental of others, because we always seem to be pouncing on wounded Christians. For several years, when my schedule permits, I have been teaching a Bible class on a weekly basis at a rehabilitation center for men with drug and alcohol problems and all the other issues resulting from addiction. These men represent all age groups, multiple professions, and all levels of society. Some have graduate degrees and held executive positions in business; others didn't finish elementary school. Some grew up in exclusive neighborhoods as members of affluent families; others have known only poverty and homelessness. Some are well groomed and manicured and dressed in expensive clothing; others are decorated with multiple tattoos and body piercing and they are dressed in rejects from the Salvation Army. Some have never even received a traffic ticket; others are ex-convicts. Yet, they are all on the same level and speak the same language when dealing with their problems. They are open and frank with each other when they relate what was going on in their life and where they were hurting and how they were struggling with their difficulties. Most of the men tell me that they would never say in a church the things they say before each other. They feel that they can be transparent in their own gatherings, because they know that nobody there will condemn them. But most of them have had the experience of having judgment and condemnation heaped upon them in church congregations.

Many people, upon hearing of a brother falling into sin, react with a haughty, "Doesn't surprise me; I didn't think he would hold out." What kind of attitude is that? If you didn't think he would hold out, where were you? Why weren't you praying for him, instructing him, encouraging him?

Others delight in gossiping about the sinning brother, gleefully smearing his deed everywhere they go, juicing it up a little more each time they tell it. Christian love never makes capital out of others' faults, nor does it delight in exposing the weakness of others. The standard of the New Testament for relationships in the Christian family is high and healthy. In all our attitudes and behavior towards others we are to be neither the judge—harsh, censorious and condemning, nor the hypocrite—blaming others while excusing ourselves—but the brother, caring for others so much that we seek to be constructive and restore them when they fall into sin.

The word translated "restore" literally means "to put in order," "to repair." In secular Greek it was often used as a medical term for setting a broken or dislocated bone. In Mark 1:19 it is used of the apostles who were "mending" their nets. We are a family, a body, and when a member of the body falls into sin it's like a part of the net being broken. We must mend the net if it's to be effective. So in dealing with a Christian in sin, we are to correct him, but not as a prosecuting attorney seeking a conviction, or as a judge exacting a penalty, but as a loving brother eager to rescue and to restore. Any other attitude toward fellow believers is an attitude of carnality that the Holy Spirit must rebuke. If you are a wise old sheep and you see a lamb that has mud on its fleece, don't push him in the mire; draw him out and tell him how to be cleansed. Notice that "you who are spiritual" are the ones to engage in the ministry of restoration. Paul is not talking about those who are the "spiritual elite," but those who are mature, taught deeply in the Word and led by the Holy Spirit. For example, Paul states in Romans 15:1: "We then who are strong ought to bear with the weaknesses of the weak, and not to please ourselves." Earlier, in Romans 14:1, he wrote that we are to accept the one who is weak in faith, but not for the purpose of passing judgment. The problem in the church is not the weak believers so much as the strong believers who are not fulfilling their responsibility of helping the weak to become stronger and restoring them when they fall.

Paul instructs that the restoration is to be done not in a spirit of condemning superiority, coming against the sinner like a prosecuting attorney and telling him how terrible he is and that the church should kick him out. We are to deal with him meekly in "a spirit of gentleness." Such gentleness is born from a sense of our own weakness and proneness to sin. Phillips translates Paul's instructions, "Not with any feeling of superiority but being yourselves on guard against temptation." In other words, we are to deal gently with someone who has fallen into sin because the very same thing can happen to us. These are dangerous words: "That will never happen to me!" The person who makes such a presumptuous assertion is a prime candidate for that very thing, because Paul elsewhere warns, "Let him who thinks he stands take heed lest he fall" (1 Cor. 10:12).

The exercise of a humble and gentle ministry of restoration certainly does not mean that we are to excuse or condone a brother's sin. On the contrary, according to the teachings of Jesus in Matthew 18:15-17, we are to go to our brother and tell him his fault, fact to face and privately. If he doesn't listen to us, then we are to take two or three others in the attempt to restore him. If he doesn't heed them, then bring the matter before the church. If he is still unheeding, then he is to be considered as an outsider, and not part of the fellowship at all. Paul gives similar instructions concerning our relationships with professing Christians who persist in known sin (1 Cor. 5:11; 2 Thess. 3:6). Christian love is always opposed to sin, and grieves and weeps over it. It is the ally of the truth, and in sheltering the sinner, seeking to restore him, it will never fail to condemn his sin.

Care for One Another

In using the analogy of the human body in 1 Corinthians 12, Paul presents one of the finest pictures in the New Testament concerning the unity of the church. In verse 25 he states that "that the members should have the same care for one another." We have already considered the physical and material concerns of Christian fellowship, but the New Testament presents other features of mutual care in "one another" relationships.

Kindness

If we truly care for one another, we will "be kind to one another" (Eph. 4:32). This quality, as well as the others mentioned in the same verse, characterizes the behavior of God and Jesus. The word is *chrestos*, and because of the obvious similarity to the name of Christ (*Christos*), Christians early recognized its peculiar appropriateness to mutual relations. Jesus used this word in describing the mercy of God when He declared, "He is kind to the unthankful and evil" (Luke 6:35). Secular Greek often used the word to describe the disposition of mind that thinks as much of others' concerns as it does of its own. It's apparent, then, that the quality of kindness will not allow us to indulge in idle selfishness and comfortable self-pleasing. Kindness leads us to be as concerned with the needs of others as we are with out own needs. Love must be kind. You can no more have love without kindness than you can have springtime without flowers. The greatest thing a person can do for the King is to be kind to the other citizens of the Kingdom. The one who has that disposition has learned the secret of looking outwards all the time, and not inwards.

Hospitality

If we care for one another, then certainly we must "be hospitable to one another without grumbling" (1 Pet. 4:9). The New Testament strongly insists on the duty of hospitality. Every Kingdom citizen is to be "given to hospitality" (Rom. 12:13). Among the many qualities of one who desires to be a bishop is that he be "hospitable" (1 Tim. 3:2; Tit. 1:8). Kingdom citizens are not to "forget to entertain strangers," because "by so doing some have unwittingly entertained angels" (Heb. 13:2). And remember that Jesus will say to those on the right hand, "I was a stranger and you took Me in," but to those on the left hand He will say, "I was a stranger and you did not take Me in" (Matt. 25:35, 43).

Hospitality was an admirable virtue in the ancient world even among non-Christians. The Jews had a saying: "There are six things, the fruit of which a man eats in this world and by which his horn is raised in the world to come." The first quality on the list is "hospitality to the stranger and visiting the sick." The pagan religions encouraged hospitality in a world in which the inns were impossibly expensive, unbelievably filthy, and notoriously immoral. The code of those religions was such that strangers, even criminals, could seek and find refuge in their temples.

The necessity for hospitality was even more evident in the circle of the Christians. Some writers have gone so far as to suggest that the early church could not have existed apart from the hospitality that Christians showed to one another. Wandering preachers and prophets were dependent on that hospitality, as were Christians traveling in the ordinary business of life, especially in areas where to be a Christian was to be an outlaw. Both their price and their immoral atmosphere made the public inns uninviting to Christians. And not to be forgotten is the fact that for two hundred years there was no such thing as a church building. Church meetings were held in the houses of those who willingly opened them for services of the congregation (see Acts 2:46; Rom. 16:5; 1 Cor. 16:19; Phm. 2).

Tyndale used a magnificent word in his version of 1 Peter 4:9. He translated it that the Christian should have a **harborous** disposition. Every Christian home should be a place of refuge, a place of refreshment and ministry, where no guest leaves unblessed.

Serving

If we want to express our care for one another, then we must "through love serve one another" (Gal. 5:13). This exhortation is set in the context of Paul's admonition to the Galatians not to turn Christian freedom into unbridled license, using it as a pretext for self-indulgence. The apostle points out that Christian freedom is not an unrestricted liberty to wallow in our own selfishness, whether that selfishness involves the indulgence of our flesh or the exploitation of our neighbor without love. Christian freedom is no more freedom to do as I please irrespective of the good of my neighbor than it is freedom to do as I please irrespective of the moral demands of Christ.

Rather than having liberty to ignore, neglect, or abuse our Christian brothers and sisters, our King commands us to love them, and through love to serve them. The New Testament will never allow us to use them as though they were **things** to serve us; it demands that we respect them as **persons** and give ourselves over to their service. In fact, the Greek word is literally "to serve as a slave," reminding us once again of the example set by our Lord in the Upper Room. Did He not tell us on that occasion that we "ought to wash one another's feet" (John 13:14)? Through love, then, we are to become each other's "slaves," not to be one master with many slaves, but each to be one slave with many masters. We are to sacrifice our good for theirs, not theirs to ours. Christian freedom is liberty to serve others, not a selfish demand to be served.

Here is another of the many paradoxes of the New Testament. Christian freedom is actually a kind of slavery—not slavery to our flesh, but to Christ (Rom. 1:1; Phil. 1:1, etc.) and to our neighbor (see 2 Cor. 4:5). So to love one another means to serve one another as a slave, and Paul proceeds to spell out some negative and positive aspects of that kind of love, some of which we have already considered, and others of which we shall consider later.

Comfort

If we care for one another, we will "comfort one another" (1 Thess. 4:18) and "comfort each other" (1 Thess. 5:11) in the time of bereavement. The Christian church is a community of mutual comfort, edification and encouragement. Bereavement is a very poignant human experience. Most of us have had the experience, and however firm our Christian faith may be, the loss of a close relative or friend causes a profound psychological and emotional shock. Not only does such a loss sometimes necessitate a very painful and radical readjustment, but it also raises some anguished questions: "What has happened to the loved one? Is he or she all right?" Such questions are understandable, whether they are asked out of curiosity, out of concern for the person who has died, or out of concern for our own security. In addition, the Thessalonians had some theological questions. They were expecting the immediate return of the Lord to claim His people and that them to Himself. Therefore, they were deeply distressed when some among their number died before Christ returned. How would they fare when Jesus came for His own? Would they be at a disadvantage?

The answers that Paul gave to these questions still bring comfort today in the midst of bereavement. In fact, it is "with these words" (1 Thess. 4:18), this doctrine, that we comfort one another. In saying this, I have not forgotten one of the lessons of the book of Job and his so-called comforters. We have to give them credit that at first, for seven days and nights, they sat in silent sympathy where he sat. And Job would probably have been better off if they had kept their mouths shut when the week ended! Instead, they drowned him in a torrent of cold, traditional words, until in the last chapter God appears and contradicts the cold comfort these men gave. Their mistake, however, was not that they talked. It was that they talked nonsense. Generally speaking, words do encourage. Words do comfort. And we can derive great comfort from Christian doctrine as we stay our minds on these truths.

So what Paul gave the Thessalonians and urged them to give to one another in their anxieties about bereavement and judgment was not soothing, words without content, but the foundation truths of the Christian gospel. He does not forbid grieving altogether. Mourning is natural and necessary. If Jesus wept over the tomb of Lazarus, then most certainly we are at liberty to do the same. What Paul forbids in 1 Thessalonians 4:13 is grieving like those who have no hope. There is a difference between Christian and non-Christian grieving. In the face of death, the pagans had no hope, but they stood in despair. They met death with grim resignation marked by bleak hopelessness. Aeschylus wrote, "Once a man dies there is no resurrection." Theocritus wrote, "There is hope for those who are alive, but those who have died are without hope." Carved on the tombstones of the ancient philosophers were such grim epitaphs as, "I was not; I became; I am not; I care not."

But Christians have a hope. It concerns the coming again of Jesus, which Paul describes with a word (*parousia*) that denotes the visit of a king. But the Christian hope is not just the coming of the King. It is that when He comes His subjects will be with Him (1 Thess. 4:14), and there will be a great reunion at the rapture (v. 17). Furthermore, the one who is coming again is the very same person who died and rose again (1 Thess. 5:9, 10). The one who is coming to complete our salvation is the one who died for us, that whether we wake or sleep we might live with Him. So when He died He overcame the two great enemies of mankind—sin and death. And if we are united to Jesus Christ, neither sin nor death can ever separate us from Him. Nothing can come between us! Look at the emphatic repetition in 4:14 and 5:10: "With Him . . . With Him." We enjoy a union with Christ that nothing, neither death, nor bereavement, nor judgment, could ever destroy. "Therefore comfort one another with these words." Remember also that God is "the Father of mercies and God of all comfort, who comforts us in all our tribulation, that we may be able to comfort those who are in any trouble, with the comfort with which we ourselves are comforted by God" (2 Cor. 1:3-4).

Bearing Burdens

If we truly care for one another, then we will not hesitate to "bear one another's burdens" (Gal. 6:2). Everybody has a burden of some kind. I heard Oral Roberts say many times, "Everybody either has a problem, is a problem, or is married to a problem!" We all have needs, and God does not want us to bear those burdens alone. Yet, some Christians try to do just that, and for various reasons. Some believers deny outright that they have burdens. "After all," they may say, "when you become a Christian, filled with the Holy Spirit, then all your problems immediately vanish. So if I admit to being burdened, that will tarnish the glory of God and cast a shadow on His goodness. Furthermore, if I admit that I have burdens, people will wonder about my spirituality and question my faith. And if I do acknowledge my burdens, then it would be a sign of weakness to confess that I can't bear them alone. So it's evidence of my fortitude not to bother other people with my burdens." Such fortitude may be admirable and brave, but it is not Christian; it is stoical.

Others may say, "But I've got a divine burden-bearer who is quite adequate, so I don't need anyone's help. Doesn't Psalm 55:22 tell us to 'cast your burden on the Lord, and He shall sustain you'? As a matter of fact, according to 1 Peter 5:7, we can cast **all** our care on the Lord, since He cares for us." But remember that God works through instruments, and one of the ways in which He bears our burdens is through human friendship.

The career of the apostle Paul provides a perfect example of the point I'm making. Do you think he was such a spiritual giant and so close to Christ that he never had any problems? Then read in 2 Corinthians 1:8 his admission of carrying a heavy burden, and his confession that it was beyond his power to handle. He said, "For we do not want you to be ignorant, brethren, of our trouble which came to us in Asia, that we were burdened beyond measure, above strength, so that we despaired of life." He then gave praise to God for his deliverance and testified that their prayers on his behalf were effective.

Later, Paul described the terrible burden he had for the Corinthian church: "Our bodies had no rest, but we were troubled on every side. Outside were conflicts, inside were fears." Then he continued: "Nevertheless, God, who comforts the downcast, comforted us by the coming of Titus" (2 Cor. 7:5-6). So God brought comfort to Paul in his distress not by the visitation of an angel and not by a mystical experience, but by the ministry of a friend, Titus.

Don't ever become so super-spiritual that you say you are above the need of human friendship. If you are that super-spiritual, then you are super-scriptural as well (see 2 Tim. 4:9). A brotherhood in which we bear one another's burdens is part of the purpose of the King for His subjects. So we should not keep our burdens to ourselves, but rather share them with Christian friends who in turn will bear them with us.

Paul states that by such burden bearing we "fulfill the law of Christ" (Gal. 6:2). We have already seen that the law of Christ is His new commandment that we love each other as He loves us (John 13:34; 15:12). Earlier, in Galatians 5:14, Paul stated that to love our neighbor as ourselves is to fulfill the law. Here then are three equivalent expressions: to "love our neighbor," to "bear one another's burdens," and to "fulfill the law." To love one another as Christ loves us may not lead us to the martyrdom of giving ourselves in a spectacular deed of self-sacrifice; it may involve the simple ministry of burden bearing. When we see someone struggling with a heavy physical load, we rush to render aid. At least we hold the door open! How much more should we share burdens of heart and mind! Bearing someone's burdens has the idea of going along and helping that person carry his load. Through sympathy and encouragement and other expressions and deeds, there are a thousand ways that you can bear one another's burdens.

If you are willing to be a burden bearer, you certainly will not lack burdens to bear. Nobody is strong enough to live the Christian life alone. All around us there are people who need someone to help. Perhaps they are under such a heavy trial they are despairing of their very lives, and they desperately need someone to come alongside and say, "Let me help. Let me pray with you. Let me just be there for you." We urgently need to be sensitive to the promptings of the Holy Spirit at this point. You may never know what your genuine smile might mean to another person, or that encouraging pat on the back, or a gentle touch, or a written note, a telephone call, or an inexpensive little gift. Sometimes just being there is all that is necessary.

I know that my Heavenly Father has all the time in the world just for me. Therefore, if I am to be like Him, I must give of myself to others. Countless times students and others would interrupt when I was a working under a tight schedule. Sometimes it was even a lowly freshman that invaded the sanctuary of my office retreat! I would act contrary to the love of Christ if I made that person feel that he was an intruder. With the Spirit of Christ in me, I could only greet that person as a brother, making him feel that at that moment he was the most important person in the world to me, and that I had nothing more pressing to do than to listen to his need and do what I could to help.

Most often, when we read Paul's letter to the Romans, we glide over the last chapter, where he expresses greetings to and from various people. As a result, we fail to grasp priceless jewels hidden therein. In particular, it's remarkable that, although Paul had never been to Rome, he appends the longest list of personal greetings found in any of his epistles. He has somehow kept track of the Christians he has met and knows their whereabouts and present circumstances. He showed a real concern for people and a genuine interest in them.

Paul implies in Galatians 6:3 that some people refuse to bear the burdens of others because they think they're too good to do it. It would be beneath their dignity to get down and grovel with somebody else and their problem. They won't demean themselves to go out into some areas and minister to somebody in great need. That attitude, of course, results from the self-conceit that we saw described in Galatians 5:26. To have that attitude, Paul says, is to be self-deceived. Some people think so highly of themselves they think they're really something, when in fact they're really nothing. Paul's evaluation is not an exaggeration—not when the Holy Spirit opens our eyes to see what we are apart from the grace of God.

Almost daily there are news reports of incidents that show the callous unconcern of people in general toward the needs of others. A disturbed man on a window ledge several stories high was threatening to jump to his death, while the crowd below jeered and taunted him, daring him to take his own life. A destitute woman, ill with pneumonia, lay unattended on a blanket on the floor of a bare apartment. All the furniture had been repossessed. The water department sent a man to the apartment to turn off the water, and he was moved to indignation by the woman's enforced suffering. Later, after she had died and there was a great outcry in the newspaper, he expressed his indignation. But he had turned off the water and had done nothing to help. It was the same with the rent collector who had thought it was such a terrible thing and something should have been done about it, and then directed the janitor to turn off the heat in the apartment "as a matter of policy." The neighbor across the hall didn't like the dead woman because she had once entertained guests and the music was too loud. Everybody was busy minding his own business, and therefore nobody bothered to practice Galatians 6:2. In stark contrast to these examples is the Christian lady who asks the local hospital to keep her informed of any patients who receive no visitors, and then visits them herself.

To be a burden bearer is to engage in a great and needed ministry. It's something that every Christian should and can do, and it's a natural consequence of walking in the Spirit. Martin Luther wrote, "Christians must have strong shoulders and mighty bones"—strong and mighty enough, that is, to carry heavy burdens.

Belonging to One Another

All this active, purposive care for one another arises from the fundamental and inescapable fact that **we belong to one another**. We are our brother's keeper precisely because we are brothers. Paul expresses it even more graphically: "So we, being many, are one body in Christ, and individually members of one another" (Rom. 12:5; see Eph. 4:25).

Interdependency

Using the analogy of a human body, in which there are many parts but an essential unity, the apostle teaches that the members of the body of Christ are mutually dependent on one another. Therefore, we must serve one another with the gifts that have been granted to us, neither envying nor despising one another, "that there should be no schism in the body, but that the members should have the same care for one another." Then, "if one member suffers, all the members suffer with it, or if one member is honored, all the members rejoice with it." (1 Cor. 25, 26).

Several years ago the top student in the graduating class at a noted Midwestern law school was a young blind man. He insisted that half the credit for his honors should go to his friend, a fellow student who was armless. They had met early in their academic career when the armless student guided the blind student down a flight of stairs. The acquaintance quickly ripened into friendship. The blind man carried the books and the armless one read aloud for their common study. Following graduation they formed a successful law partnership.

This lovely story is a true illustration of the way Christians should function together as the body of Christ. We do not all have the same gifts, but those that we do have are for the common upbuilding of all believers. Therefore, all that we possess in the way of spiritual gifts is to be put at the disposal of other believers. Only in this way can we be built up together until we come into "the measure of the stature of the fullness of Christ" (Eph. 4:13).

Living in Harmony

Our King intends that His subjects live in harmony, "endeavoring to keep the unity of the Spirit in the bond of peace" (Eph. 4:3). To be in harmony necessarily means that we will "be of the same mind toward one another" (Rom. 12:16), and more specifically, we will "be like-minded toward one another according to Christ Jesus" (Rom. 15:5). When strife and faction enter into any Christian society, its effectiveness for service in the Kingdom of God is severely limited and its witness to the outside world is drastically crippled. However architecturally ornate the building may be in which a congregation meets, however pleasing its worship and its music, however generous its giving, if it has no harmony, it does not possess the essential of Christian fellowship. To be in harmony does not mean that there cannot be differences of opinion about certain issues, but it does mean that those who have learned what it is to live in fellowship know that the Christ who unites them is far greater than the differences that may divide them. The glory of Christ and the good of the body as a whole take precedence over individual preferences. As a result, "with one mind and one mouth" we are able to "glorify the God and Father of our Lord Jesus Christ" (Rom. 15:6).

Fellow Feelings

Furthermore, being of the same mind enables us to "rejoice with those who rejoice, and weep with those who weep" (Rom. 12:15). In commenting on this passage, Chrysostom, the great Christian preacher and theologian of the fourth century, wrote: "It requires more of a high Christian temper to rejoice with them that do rejoice than to weep with them that weep. For this nature itself fulfills perfectly; and there is none so hard-hearted as not to weep over him that is in calamity; but the other requires a very noble soul, so as not only to keep from envying, but even to feel pleasure with the person who is in esteem." What he meant is that it's more difficult to congratulate another person on his success (especially if his success involves disappointment to us), than it is to sympathize with his sorrow. Being of the same mind and dead to self, we can rejoice as much in the success of others as in our own. The moment we become a Christian, our lives are to cease to be self-centered, and we are to become characterized by one-anotherness. Then the feelings of our brothers and sisters become more important than our own, which is simply a reflection of the practice of putting others first and self last.

The Source of Our Oneness

As we have previously noted, we derive our oneness from a common experience of Jesus Christ and a common allegiance to Him. Life in Christ sweeps out all narrowness and pettiness and selfishness and censoriousness and creates a fellowship that is radiant and released and exultant and contagious. Therefore, if there is something impeding the one-mindedness of the fellowship, we need to go back to the source of unity—to Christ. On one occasion disaffection and disunity broke out among the men of Napoleon's Old Guard, and the risk was great. But Napoleon knew how to meet the crisis. He sat alone in a little room in his palace, a room that had two large apartments opening off it to the right and to the left.

In the hall to the left the members of the Guard were assembled. Napoleon summoned each man alone into his presence. When each one entered the room and closed the door, Napoleon did not speak a single word. He merely clasped the man's hand and looked him full in the face. Then each man exited by the door on the right, until the whole of the Guard, one by one, had passed through. After they all had gone through the room, the disaffection and disunity were over. The silent look and the handclasp had done their work. Every one of them was Napoleon's now, and thus all were one with each other in their single-minded devotion. Can it not be the same with us one by one as we look into the face of our Commander Jesus, with His hand, pierced with the nail, clasping ours?

John Fawcett wrote these words in 1782, and Christians have been singing them ever since:

Blest be the tie that binds

Our hearts in Christian love:

The fellowship of kindred minds

Is like to that above.

Before our Father's throne

We pour our ardent prayers;

Our fears, our hopes, our aims, are one,

Our comforts and our cares.

This "fellowship of kindred minds" is the church.

Granting Forgiveness

To be in harmony means that we will not harbor ill will of any kind toward other members of the family, whether it's bitterness, unforgiveness, vengeance, or any such attitude. On the contrary, we will be like Christ in "forgiving one another" (Col. 3:13; Eph. 4:32). An unforgiving spirit is the devil's playground and the Christian's battleground. If someone hurts us, either deliberately or unintentionally, and we do not practice forgiveness, then we begin to develop a bitterness that soon hardens the heart, destroying not only our relationship with the other person, but with the Father. Actually, we are not hurting the person who wronged us; we are only hurting ourselves, allowing a cancerous sore to fester inside us.

One of the easiest things in the world to do is to justify ourselves. Actually, self-justification is just as strong an urge as self-preservation. We rush to our own defense when we suffer criticism, and we can easily excuse an attitude of unforgiveness and feel most righteous about it. "You don't know what he did to me!" we cry. "You don't know what she said about me! I have a right to feel this way!"

Perhaps someone has wronged you, and perhaps you do have a right to harbor bad feelings toward the person who hurt you, but would you rather be "right" and continue in misery, or forgive and have the joy of the Lord? You see, bitterness in the heart makes us treat others the way Satan treats them; whereas we should treat others the way God has treated us. In His gracious kindness, God has forgiven us, and we should forgive others. We do not forgive for our sake, although we do get a blessing from it, or even for their sake, but for Jesus' sake. Learning how to forgive and forget is one of the secrets of a joyful Christian life.

Some years ago I led a team on a mission trip of several weeks to Mexico and Central America. (And I want to state most emphatically that **I** was the leader!) Unfortunately, the team didn't always appreciate my decisions. In fact, there was outright mutiny. Well, I showed them! I withdrew into my self-righteous shell and sulked alone. But I had the satisfaction of knowing that I was right in feeling as I did. It was strange, though, that nobody seemed affected in the least by my bitterness. My self-pitying isolation didn't seem to bother them at all. If I was so right, why was I so miserable? I couldn't even pray. But in His mercy, God gently showed me that I could persist in my attitude and feel "right," or I could forgive any supposed wrong done me and experience restoration both with them and with Him. I'm glad to say that I chose the latter course. And do you know what? As I reflected on the situation later, I discovered that I had not been wronged at all. It was only that my injured ego blinded me to wiser judgment.

We have seen in 1 Corinthians 13:5 that love does not keep an account of wrongs done to it. Paul used a business term for entering an item in a ledger so it won't be forgotten. The statement simply means that, whereas love keeps a diary of all the good it receives, it does not keep a record of the wrongs done to it, concentrating on them until it's impossible to forget them. Love doesn't store in its memory the wrongs that others have inflicted on it, with the intention of getting even with them some day. It's tragic to find David on his deathbed recalling the wrongs that Joab had done him, and hearing again the curses of Shimei showered upon him as he fled from Jerusalem. He had written down all those things in his account books, but love does not keep such records. Love is generous in its forgetfulness. Actually, the old human nature finds it difficult, if not impossible, to forget wrongs, and the advice to "forgive and forget" finds little acceptance among us. How can we forget the terrible pain and damage that callous, insensitive, vindictive people have inflicted upon us? In the final analysis, perhaps only God has the ability to forget. But it's a greater testimony to the grace of God in your heart when you can say, "I remember what that person did, but I forgive him. It's no longer an issue; it doesn't matter."

In a figurative sense, all of us, whether we know it or not, carry a ledger book around with us. In it we keep an account of all the wrongs done against us. "I'm writing down that false statement that Mrs. Jones said about me." "I've got a grudge against the pastor because he didn't call on me." Forgiveness is ripping out all the pages of that book, tearing them to shreds and saying, "They don't owe me a thing. They may have wronged me, they may have harmed me, but I forgive."

It is said of Abraham Lincoln that he never forgot a kindness, and that he had no room in his mind for the memory of a wrong. There is a morality of memory, and love keeps a list of its creditors, but none of its debtors. Imagine my amazement and dismay at the attitude of a professing Christian woman whom I had instructed concerning the need to forgive someone who had supposedly wronged her. I urged upon her the necessity of not only forgiving but also taking the initiative to bring about reconciliation and thus a restoration of their fellowship. Her reply was, "Oh, I have forgiven her, but she had better stay in her place and not show herself around here again."

Jesus taught, "When you pray, say . . . we also forgive everyone who is indebted to us" (Luke 11:2-4). Forgiving without forgetting is like a vulture feeding on a dead carcass, until even the breath of prayer smells of the putrid thing.

Jesus also said, "If you do not forgive men their trespasses, neither will your Father forgive your trespasses" (Matt. 6:15). The horrible sin of unforgiveness is a blight upon our Christian life that can rob us of the joy of the Lord. It's a deadly poison that causes everything from mental depression to health problems. It can block the free flow of communion with the King and it can embitter all of the relationships of life. Unforgiveness is one of the devil's favorite and most effective weapons of mass destruction.

One of America's finest poets was Edwin Markham. At one period in his life he lost his inspiration and could not compose poetry. What had happened was that a business partner had terribly wronged him. Unable to forgive the man for the hurt inflicted upon him, Markham brooded over the injury until his bitterness robbed him of the ability to write. Finally, God's grace enabled him to express forgiveness for the man who had cheated him. In the vast relief that engulfed him upon forgiving his former partner, Markham sat down and wrote his famous couplet entitled "Outwitted":

> He drew a circle that shut me out,
>
> Heretic, rebel, a thing to flout.
>
> But love and I had the wit to win,
>
> For we drew a circle that took him in.

Forbearance

Living in harmony also demands that we be "bearing with one another" (Col. 3:13; Eph. 4:2). Forbearance is patience with people, even those who are aggravating. Chrysostom defined it as the characteristic of the man who has the power to revenge himself and who does not. It is the spirit of the person who could wipe out someone who hurts and insults him, but who is patient mercy stays his hand. Paul adds in Ephesians 4:2 that we are to practice our forbearance "in love," and in 1 Corinthians 13:4 he says that "love suffers long," the very same word translated "forbearance" elsewhere. The word denotes the long waiting time during which the wronged person refuses to give way to anger. It implies victory over resentment. Love is longsuffering when, in the face of injuries and wrongs, it persists and endures and waits without plotting retaliation.

The most illuminating thing about the word forbearance is that the New Testament commonly uses it to describe the attitude of

God and of Jesus towards people. Paul asks the impenitent sinner with mock incredulity: "Do you despise the riches of His goodness, forbearance, and longsuffering?" (Rom. 2:4). He declares that God has endured with much forbearance "the vessels of wrath prepared for destruction" (Rom. 9:22). He speaks of the perfect longsuffering of Jesus to him (1 Tim. 1:16). Peter describes the forbearance of God waiting in the days of Noah (1 Pet. 3:20), and he says that the longsuffering of God is our salvation (2 Pet. 3:15). If God had acted as man, He would have wiped us out long ago, but God has the kind of patience that bears with us in all out shortcomings, and He will not cast us off. Remember the example of Jesus, "who, when He was reviled, did not revile in return; when He suffered, He did not threaten" (1 Pet. 2:23). In our attitude toward and dealings with our fellow Christians, we must reproduce this same loving, forbearing, forgiving, patient attitude of Christ towards ourselves.

Perhaps it would help us at this point to remind ourselves that the church is not a fellowship of perfected saints, but of forgiven sinners. Our fellow believers are all imperfect, and at times they are sure to try us. There will be some in the fellowship who "get on our nerves"; others whose peculiarities annoy us; some we do not "like." Hence, there will always be the need for self-control, for patience, for forgiveness, for forbearance. Remember also that we too probably get on other people's nerves, and they have to make allowances for us. Try to appreciate the difficulties of others, pray for those you do not like, and seek if possible to help them. Avoid small-mindedness and pettiness as unworthy of "the grace of the Lord Jesus Christ."

Mutual Submission

Harmonious relationships can be fostered only in the atmosphere of "submitting to one another in the fear of God" (Eph. 5:21). This exhortation is quite similar to that given by Paul in Romans 12:10, where he calls upon us to give preference to one another. Certainly it demands the same attitude on our part of foregoing our own interests for the sake of others.

The idea of subjection to anybody or anything is out of fashion in today's "me first" society, and it's totally at variance with contemporary attitudes of permissiveness and freedom. Therefore, it's important to understand exactly what Paul means when he tells us to practice mutual submissiveness.

In Ephesians 5:18 Paul gives the command to be filled with the Spirit, and then he proceeds to show that being filled with the Spirit manifests itself in worship, praise and joy. But he makes it clear that being filled with the Spirit affects not only our relationship with God, but our relationship with one another as well. The fullness of the Holy Spirit is not merely a private, mystical experience; it definitely has its corporate aspects. In fact, everywhere in the New Testament that an exhortation is given to be filled with the Spirit or to walk in the Spirit, immediately the topic turns to relationships with other Christians.

But what exactly does it mean to be subject to one another? Basic to the meaning of Paul's directive is the recognition that in Christ, while we are still individuals, we are not individualistic. We are like soldiers in a regiment or players on a team. This recognition, and its acceptance, will express itself both negatively and positively.

Negatively, it means that my actions will not be governed by thoughtless inconsideration and unconcern with respect to the position and the needs and the desires and the welfare of others. Nor will I be so self-centered and self-assertive that I become opinionated to the extent that I dictatorially lord my opinions over others, impatiently dismissing other points of view.

Earlier I mentioned an extended mission outreach that I led throughout Mexico and Central America. As I reflected later on the schism that developed, I saw that the basic cause of the dissension was that anyone should dare question my judgment. I was so proud of my opinions that I would not entertain any opposing ideas. For anyone to propose something to the contrary was a gross insult to me—not to the truth, but to me. What mattered was what I believed, and I didn't want to hear anything else.

Self-centeredness is a deadly and disruptive disease, and its symptoms are legion. It affects every part of a person's being—his thinking, his emotions, his action, his will, his outlook. A self-centered person takes criticism, even well meant, as a sign of distrust and a lack of appreciation. So if he doesn't get his own way, he'll take his ball and go home; he'll resign from the committee; he'll walk off the stage in a huff.

Subjection to one another expresses itself positively in the opposite way. It recognizes the fact that we are like the different parts and members of a body. That recognition leads to a further realization that what really is important is not so much that you are a part, but that you are a part of a whole, and that it is the whole that matters and not the part. In other words, it will lead you to a consideration of the body and its good, not just your own personal good.

The Christian who realize these things will be ready to forego his individualistic rights. As he contemplates the great privilege of being a part of the body of Christ, he will be interested in the advancement of every other part also, because he knows that the advancement of the whole means his own development. So he doesn't worry about his own rights any longer, jealously watching over them and guarding them. He is ready to listen and learn. Instead of wanting to argue and quarrel, when it's not a matter of principle, he will let others have their way. Filled with the Spirit, he will not want to lift up himself above others, but to serve others.

Furthermore, he is ready to suffer, unjustly if necessary, for the sake of the body of Christ. He puts into practice the virtues of love as described in 1 Corinthians 13. He submits himself readily and willingly for the sake of others and for the good of the whole cause. The Spirit in us is the Spirit of Jesus, and Jesus, with no taint of sin in Him, submitted Himself to wicked men, even to the cross.

I firmly believe that most of the petty things that disrupt harmony in our churches would disappear if we would only realize that the gospel reduces every one of us to the same level. Paul states this truth superbly in writing to the Corinthians who were boasting of their gifts and wisdom: "For who differ from another? And what do you have that you did not receive? Now if you did indeed receive it, why do you boast as if you had not received it?" (1 Cor. 4:7). So you have a great brain, or good looks, or some unusual talent—but where did you get it? The moment you realize that all these things are gifts, you stop boasting. To do otherwise is to be worldly. The world grades people on looks, talent and ability. It offers honors and prizes, causing people to flush with pride and with their earthly success. How different is the biblical outlook!

Seeking Forgiveness

Because mutual offenses against one another create a breach in harmonious relationships, the King instructs us to "confess your trespasses to one another" (James 5:16). It's true that all misdeeds are sins against God, but it is also true that some are sins as well against our fellow Kingdom citizens. Therefore, when our sin has offended others as well as God, we must confess to them and seek forgiveness from them also. We must say to the injured party, in the prodigal's words to his father: "I have sinned against heaven and against you" (Luke 15:21 NIV). The principle is clear—we must seek forgiveness from the one whom we have offended; we must confess to the one from whom we seek forgiveness.

Throughout this study we have stressed that the Bible teaches the importance of right relations with others, and that a right relationship with God is impossible without them. The prophets of the seventh and eighth centuries B.C. constantly preached this theme. They declared that the offering of sacrifices to God was not only useless; it was positively nauseating to Him if the worshippers were living lives of immorality or injustice to others (see Isa. 1:13-17; 59:1-19; Hosea 6:6; Amos 5:21-24; Micah 6:6-8, etc.).

Jesus echoed the teachings of the prophets in the Sermon on the Mount: "Therefore if you bring your gift to the altar, and there remember that your brother has something against you, leave your gift there before the altar, and go your way. First be reconciled to your brother, and then come and offer your gift" (Matt. 5:23-24). The situation is obvious. We are in the middle of a worship service, offering praise to the Lord, when suddenly we remember somebody who has a grievance against us. It's not that he has wronged us, but that we have offended him. The teaching of Jesus makes it clear that it's no use trying to worship when such a sin comes to our mind and burdens our conscience. How can we draw near to God while we are estranged from a brother? We are not even to wait until the service is over; we are to leave at once and put the matter right. The command is "first go . . . then come . . ." "First be reconciled to your brother" (which means "ask for his forgiveness"), and then your offering will be acceptable to God.

A word of caution is in order here. All sins, whether of thought, word, or deed, must be confessed to God, because He sees them all—thoughts, ways and words (Psa. 139:1-4). But remember that while others can hear our words and see our works, they cannot read our hidden thoughts. To confess to others sinful thoughts we have harbored about them may embarrass rather than help. For example, Jesus taught, "Whoever looks at a woman to lust for her has already committed adultery with her in his heart" (Matt. 5:28). It ought to be obvious that this is adultery in the sight of God and that it is to be confessed to Him, not to the woman involved. A good guide is to confess secret sins secretly (to God), and private sins privately (to the injured party). Any sin that hinders the worship of the church and inhibits the fellowship of its members ought to be confessed so that right relationships both with God and with one another might be restored. But there is no basis here for systematically blurting out every evil thought and bad intention toward a brother or a sister.

Sincere Honesty

However, confession within the framework of Christian fellowship involves more than the acknowledgement of having offended someone. It includes a certain honesty, a word seldom found in a theological wordbook. Fellowship is more than a warm feeling of personal affinity, which tends to be merely sentimental. It involves a mutual sharing of the realities about each other—knowing and being known. Let me illustrate what I mean. A group of housewives had been meeting regularly for Bible study, but there was an evident lack of spiritual growth in the group. Finally, one day after she had led the study, the teacher spontaneously began confessing to the other women that she had not been living up to the marvelous truths that she had been talking about. Her embarrassment was only exceeded by her surprise when one of the others began unburdening herself also, sharing her failures and needs with the group. Another woman did the same, and another, as the freedom to drop their masks became contagious and spread from person to person. In the midst of acknowledging their own shortcomings, they discovered that others in the group were strong where they were weak. Thus, they were able to minister to one another by sharing the divine resources made available through the Holy Spirit—resources made doubly powerful in a supporting fellowship.

Honesty is the tonic of fellowship, keeping it from becoming soft and squashy. Truth will change mere congeniality into genuine fellowship, intellectual discussion into personal sharing, and talking about the Christian life into experiencing it together. However, being honest about oneself to promote fellowship is very costly. The chief cost is the willingness to bear the pain of giving and receiving the corrective of the truth. Fellowship can become a counterfeit in two ways—when we refuse to be honest with others as we see them doing a wrong thing, or a right thing in a wrong way; or when we refuse to receive from them the same honesty concerning our own needs. "Speaking the truth in love" is not only an apostolic command; it is the only way to foster human relations. No relationship is healthy without the element of loving honesty.

Of course, this kind of honesty must work both ways. If we speak candidly to others but refuse to receive candid words from them, we are dominating. If we receive candid words but refuse to speak them, we are doormats. We must deal in the truth spoken in love (not in cruel and brutal frankness), receiving it from others even if it hurts, and giving it to them even if it costs us to do so. However, if the cost is great, the rewards are also great, not the least of which is the exchange of counterfeit Christian fellowship for the real thing.

Praying for One Another

People living in harmony will not neglect to "pray for one another" (James 5:16). Reinforcements of grace and power and fortitude always arrive when earnest intercession prevails. Within the household of faith we would all face challenges with greater daring, and live with a more hopeful and patient and enterprising spirit, if we had the assurance that others were in constant prayer for us. Jesus thought it worthwhile to tell Peter that He was praying for him (Luke 22:32), and the intercessory prayer of John 17 contains some of the noblest words of the Lord that are recorded in the Bible.

Paul constantly gave assurance to others that he was faithful in his prayers for them (Eph. 1:16; Phil. 1:4; Col. 1:3, 9; 2 Tim. 1:3, etc.), and, as we have noted earlier, he genuinely desired their prayers for him.

We display an egocentric uncharitable attitude if we withhold our prayers for others, and we reveal a presumptuous conceit if we think we don't need the prayers of others for us. How can we refuse to give or receive intercessory prayer when we realize that the greatest of all saints was constant in intercession for others and was not ashamed to ask for the prayers of the least of the brethren. Tennyson wrote:

More things are wrought by prayer

Than this world dreams of. Wherefore, let thy voice

Rise like a fountain for me night and day.

For what are men better than sheep or goats

That nourish a blind life within the brain,

If, knowing God, they lift not hands of prayer

Both for themselves and those who call them friend?

Bond by gold chains about the feet of God.

Epaphras set a fine example for prayer within the fellowship. He was a member of the church at Colossae, and Paul assured the Christians there that Epaphras was "always laboring fervently for you in prayers" (Col. 4:12). I once met an elderly couple who were not able to participate in many of the activities of the church, but who could pray. Not only were they constant in prayer for the pastor and other members of the church; their concern reached even farther. Every day they would read through the newspaper. They read the notices of the births and prayed for the babies; they read the announcements of marriages and prayed that the new homes would be prosperous and Christ-centered; they read the obituaries and prayed that the sorrowing would be comforted; they read the hospital reports and prayed for healing. Who can tell the released power that flowed from that home to the ends of the earth?

I am convinced that Kingdom *koinonia* would be vastly enriched and deepened if we prayed more often and more fervently for one another. In such a fellowship as that, not only would bodies be healed, as James indicated, but relationships as well. Dislikes and distrusts would evaporate; besetting sins would lose their power; failings of temper and faults of conduct would be overcome in the midst of those who express loving concern through faithful supplication.

Greetings of Peace

Harmonious fellowship is also displayed when we "greet one another with a holy kiss" (Rom. 16:16; 1 Cor. 16:20; 2 Cor. 13:12; 1 Pet. 5:14; see 1 Thess. 5:26). Unfortunately, this instruction is generally reduced today to nothing more than a call to a casual greeting, to such an extent that Phillips translates it "a handshake all around, please." However, this feature of fellowship involves much more than a reflection of cultural practices of the first century. The early Christians called it the kiss of peace, and for centuries it was an integral and precious part of Christian fellowship and worship.

To the Jews the kiss was a greeting of welcome and respect, the value of which may be seen in the reaction of Jesus when He was denied it (Luke 7:45). In the early church the kiss was given at the end of the prayers and just before the worshippers partook of communion. Tertullian, writing in the second century, asked: "What prayer is complete from which the holy kiss is divorced? What kind of sacrifice is that from which men depart without the peace?"

Augustine said that when Christians were about to partake of communion, "they demonstrated their inward peace by the outward kiss." Here was the sign and symbol that they sat at the table of love joined together in perfect love, having forgiven and forgotten all wrongs. In giving and receiving the kiss, they were confessing unfeigned love for one another, undefiled by hypocrisy or deceit, and they were acknowledging their oneness in the Lord.

The kiss of greeting was not restricted, however, to the observance of the Lord's Supper. Newly baptized converts were welcomed into the fellowship with the kisses of the congregation, and newly ordained ministers were given "the kiss in the Lord." It was not given promiscuously, but because of misinterpretation by heathen slanderers, it was later confined to those of the same sex.

Although the custom is still retained among some Christians (in Russia, for example, where the men kiss the men on the lips, and the women greet one another likewise), it faded when the church became less and less of a fellowship. As congregations grew and became more scattered, so that members did not know one another, and often did not wish to know each other, the intimacy was lost. I pray that it will not take the persecution that some are enduring to bring us back into the reality of fellowship.

Joy in One-Anotherness

Jesus connected the fullness of joy with loving one another (John 15:11-12). The apostle Paul stated that "none of us lives to himself" (Rom. 14:7). We are all bound up together in the intricate bundle of our complex life, and our attitude toward one-anotherness determines whether we have heaven below or hell of earth. If the fullness of joy comes through loving one another, then most people are sadly mistaken. They think that joy comes by putting self first, and it is this mistake that lies behind the worship of wealth, the passion for power, and the pursuit of pleasure. Actually, egoism is the supreme enemy of true joy, and for that matter, of true fellowship. As we have seen, no one can function properly in the body of Christ as an egoist. The Spirit of God works in the human heart the supreme transition from selfishness to one-anotherness. "One man," says an old Latin proverb, "is no man at all." Another old saying declares, "A man wrapped up in himself makes a mighty small package." A life that is always getting and never giving is a Dead Sea.

One will never have to seek the joy that comes from giving oneself for the sake of others; it will come when the gift is made. In some self-forgetting hour when we are touched by another's need, and we sacrifice to render aid, we suddenly find our hearts aflame with a glorious joy that has come unsought. It is thus that we come to know a like joy to that of Christ Himself, for the passage in John 15 speaks of **His** joy in us. In self-sacrificing service for others we behold the prints of His sandals, and we follow in the steps of His example and share His joy. You need not roam to and fro to find glory. The secret of pure joy lies in the simple matter of one-anotherness.

Learning from Jesus

The various attitudes we have discussed in connection with one-anotherness are reflections of the character of Jesus Christ. The love of Jesus led Him to self-denying obedience to the Father's will and to self-forgetting sacrifice for those He had come to save. He came, and lived, and wrought, and suffered and died, and rose, and lived again, **for others**. His crucifiers were uttering a truth infinitely more profound than they guessed when they said, "He saved others; Himself He cannot save" (Matt. 27:42).

Jesus is the great example of longsuffering, infinitely patient because eternal. Peter summarized the Lord's habit of life by testifying that He "went about doing good" (Acts 10:38). Jesus never desired to possess any good for Himself alone; neither did He ever begrudge others any good that they possessed. He was never guilty of envy.

The Lord displayed His greatness just as much in what he suppressed as in what He exhibited, such as in the veiling of His glory and in His restraint in working miracles. In other words, there was no self-aggrandizing "showing off," as we are prone to do. He displayed no vanity, conceit, pride, or contempt of others.

Christ was the very negation of selfishness. He lived for others. He was never exasperated at wrong done to Himself, and there was much. He was never vindictive. He never retaliated. He had the divine power of forgetfulness of wrongs done to Himself.

He yearned over the erring and sinful, and He shielded them from those who would make capital of their sin. He patiently bore the wrong done Him by honor and love withheld; and at the same time He put His shoulder under the load that others were carrying and helped them carry it. He never misjudged, because He did not judge by the outward appearance. He never abandoned anybody; he hoped for and won the prodigal, the harlot and the thief. He calmly endured all opposition and persecution, and He prayed on the cross for His enemies.

The business of our lives is to manifest these characteristics in our own relationships with others. This is our prime objective in relating to others in the fellowship. If we are successful, then our fellowship on earth is a true foretaste of the fellowship we will enjoy in heaven.

VI

MAINTAINING KINGDOM UNITY

Several years ago a graduate student wrote an unusual thesis in the field of social studies. What made his work so different was that he did not carry out his research by bending over musty books in the cloistered halls of a university library. Instead, he lived the adventurous life of a hobo, riding the rails and sharing the campfires of hobo jungles across the country. One of the most interesting revelations that resulted from his experiences concerned the type of relationships that commonly existed in the groups. The student found that despite the mutual concerns and camaraderie outwardly displayed in the hobo bands, each person lived an individual existence, with not a shred of trust for the other person. The student graphically illustrated this distrust by describing the caution necessary in common conversation and in protecting one's person and property.

This experience is a vivid picture of the hopeless division that exists among people by nature. The sinful human race is a mass of prejudice, and disunity is the inevitable result. Contemporary society is still full of the kind of racial prejudice that characterized Jews and Gentiles in the ancient world. People do not hesitate to dismiss with sarcasm and scorn whole groups or nations. All of humanity is divided up in this way. Individual is divided from individual; class from class; nation from nation; Gentile from Jew. The world apart from Christ is a divided, disunited, fragmentized world. That division is not something merely superficial; it is something elemental deep down in the life of humankind. It's possible for people to put on a show and keep up appearances, while beneath there is enmity and disunion, and the mere fact that they are smiling and shaking hands does not necessarily tell you anything about their hearts. A veneer of gentleness or politeness often covers up curses in the inner person. All of us are familiar with this type of dealing. The whole so-called art of politics, whether local or international, is based upon the supposition that you cannot trust anybody, but that you must be concerned about your own best interests, making concessions when it suits you.

The King's Provision for Unity

That kind of disunity is not God's purpose. His design in creation is that the universe is a harmony and not a disharmony, and this disunity can only become a unity, and this disharmony can only become a harmony, when there is a radical change in individual lives. And what need to be changed in every one of us by nature are our very constitutions, not just what we do on the surface for the sake of appearances. It is a total waste of time to speak about unity apart from new life in Jesus Christ. Sin has fractured human fellowship, and sin will keep on fracturing it no matter how desperately people without Christ struggle to achieve a relationship of love and trust and service among themselves. Our most heroic efforts toward achieving unity totally on the human level end in dismal failure. We do not find life-fulfilling fellowship in our lodges, our clubs and our associations. At best all of these institutions offer a sham fellowship—a relation of pseudo love, without unity of heart and mind and purpose. Something is lacking in all of these efforts, and they end with futility compounded by futility. Without Jesus Christ human fellowship is like dough without yeast or like a light bulb without electricity. An important ingredient is missing. And Paul tells us what the missing element is in Ephesians 2:14-18, as he discusses the enmity between Jew and Gentile:

> For He Himself is our peace, who has made both one, and has broken down the middle wall of separation, having abolished

> in His flesh the enmity, that is, the law of commandments contained in ordinances, so as to create in Himself one new man from the two, thus making peace, and that He might reconcile them both to God in one body through the cross, thereby putting to death the enmity. And He came and preached peace to you who were afar off and to those who were near. For through Him we both have access by one Spirit to the Father.

How can traditional enemies be fused into a fellowship of life and love and light? The only mortar that can hold people together in loving fellowship is the mortar mixed with the blood that Christ shed at the cross. God's purpose at Calvary was not only to change the lives of individuals, but also to build up a new society. And that is exactly what happened. The early Christian movement included an ex-medium, an erstwhile jailer, a Roman proconsul, merchants with a big, worldwide business, a leading rabbi, the most respected leader in Jerusalem rich and poor, slave and free, male and female, all bound into a new community because they had been accepted by God for Christ's sake. All had been blessed with a love they had done nothing to deserve and could never repay—the love that took Christ to the cross. They described their new society as a temple built on the foundation of Jesus Christ, with every member a stone in the temple, related alike to the foundation and to all the other stones. They also described it as a body in which every limb had its different function, but the whole organism harmoniously served the purposes of the risen and ascended Head.

All who are truly Kingdom citizens, therefore, are of necessity one because they have recognized certain facts and have entered into certain experiences. They have admitted that they are all equally sinful; they have realized their helplessness to save themselves from sin; they have all come to the one and the same Savior; they have experienced the same salvation made possible through the blood of

Christ; they are indwelt by the same Holy Spirit; they are children of the same Father; they are marching together to the same eternal home as a company of redeemed people. I am speaking both of unity **within** churches and **between** churches. It ought to be evident, then, that the unity of God's people is not necessarily one of organization and administration. All the efforts of those who seek the structural union of Christendom through committee rooms will prove fruitless. The oneness of Christians can only be the result of supernatural activity.

In Ephesians 4:4-6 the word "one" occurs seven times. Three times the word refers to the Trinity—one Spirit (v. 4); one Lord (v. 5); and one God and Father (v. 6). The remaining uses of the word allude to our Christian experience as related to the three persons of the Trinity. This passage shows how the unity of our Christian experience arises out of the unity of our God. Let me simplify by stating three affirmations:

There is one body because there is one Spirit (v. 4). There is only one Holy Spirit, and if He dwells in you and you and you and you—and me—then of course we are one. The one Spirit animates the one body. And there is only one Spirit indwelling and animating the body. Elsewhere Paul writes, "For by one Spirit we were all baptized into one body—whether Jews or Greeks, whether slaves or free—and have all been made to drink into one Spirit" (1 Cor. 12:13).

There is one hope, one faith and one baptism, because there is only one Lord (vs. 4-5). What is the object of our faith? Jesus Christ. So there is only one faith, because there is only one Lord in whom we all believe. Again, what is the object of our baptism? We are baptized into Jesus Christ. There is only one baptism, because there is only one Christ into whom we are baptized. And what is the object of our hope? Jesus Christ, and His coming again in glory. So there is only one hope because there is only one Christ, for whom we are waiting. There is only one faith, hope and baptism, because there is only one Lord Jesus, who is the object of all three.

There is only one family, embracing us all, because there is only "one God and Father of all, who is above all, and through all, and in you all" (v. 6). So, to put it the other way around, the one Father creates the one family; the one Lord Jesus creates the one faith, hope and baptism; and the one Holy Spirit creates the one body. There **can** be only one Christian family; and there **can** be only one Christian faith, hope and baptism; and there **can** be only one body—because of the simple fact that there is only one God. The unity of the church is just as unassailable as the unity of God Himself. The church **is** one.

Unity and Disunity

At this point some will immediately raise objections. "In light of what you have just written, is the quest for the visible unity of the church a false and useless endeavor? If the church is indestructibly one, is there any need to bother about our apparent disunities? How can we reconcile the biblical teaching upon the fact of unity with the disunity that we see all around us in the church? How can you account for the fact that there are scores of denominations and hundreds of separated and competing churches?"

To answer those questions it is necessary to draw a distinction between the church's unity as an invisible reality in the mind and the sight of God, and the church's disunity as a visible appearance, contradicting the invisible reality. The Bible insists that there is only **one** Christian family, and we sense the truth of that insistence in interdenominational meetings where the participants have gathered in the name of Jesus. I speak each year in many of such gatherings, where dozens of denominations are represented, and there is among them a strength of unity that transcends whatever barriers may exist among the various denominations.

Does it sound paradoxical to speak of unity in the midst of apparent disunity? The apostle Paul recognized the possibility of disunity and dealt with it in the very passage where he so emphatically asserted the unity of the church. In Ephesians 4:3 he declared that Christians are to endeavor "to keep the unity of the Spirit in the bond of peace." The New English Bible translates, "Spare no effort to make fast with bonds of peace the unity which the Spirit gives." On the surface this exhortation appears to be very strange indeed. How can Paul urge us to maintain something that he says is indestructible? Besides, if there is a unity of the Spirit, created and maintained by the Spirit, what is the sense of urging **us** to maintain the unity of the Spirit? Quite simply, the answer is that we are to preserve this unity in visible fashion. The church **is** one; therefore it must **be** one. The oneness of believers in Christ is already a spiritual reality, but we have a responsibility to guard, protect and preserve that unity. Paul's exhortation is not that we produce a unity, not to create a unity, not to try to arrive at a unity, but to "keep the unity." The unity that the Holy Spirit creates and that exists in the mind of God must somehow show itself in the visible church. We are to preserve in actual, concrete realities of love that unity that God has created, thereby demonstrating to the world that the unity we claim exists is not empty grandiloquence, but a solid and glorious fact. It is imperative for the church to manifest outwardly this essential unity, for, as we shall see, this is to be the means of evangelizing the world (John 17:21).

The word translated "endeavoring" in Ephesians 4:3 is very emphatic. Its original meaning is "to make haste." The word means that we are to put forth an earnest, all-out effort, and the fact that the verb is in the present tense calls for a constant, persistent action. In other words, Paul calls for an urgent initiative that involves deliberate haste, concentrated endeavor, and whole-hearted effort. "Get started now! Give it your best! And keep it going!" Someone has well said that marriages may be made in heaven, but the maintenance work is done on earth. It's the same way with Christian unity. Created by God in heaven, it must be maintained by believers on earth.

But how can we perform this maintenance work? In Ephesians 4:3 the apostle declares that we are to do it "in" (or "by") the bond of peace, that is, by living in peace with one another. Previously, we have considered those qualities that promote fellowship, such as love and the positives and negatives of one-anotherness. However, there are some other practical features that contribute greatly to the maintaining of Christian unity.

Charitable Conduct

A person entering into a society automatically assumes the obligation to live in such a way as to promote the aims of that society. In the context of his exhortation to maintain unity, Paul lists five great Christian graces that we are to display if the unity of the church is to be visible: humility, gentleness, longsuffering, forbearance and love (Eph. 4:2). Since we have already discussed the last three of these five virtues elsewhere in our study of fellowship, in this context let's give attention only to the first two.

Humility, or "lowliness," is a word to which Christianity gave a new meaning. The Greeks never used the word in a good sense. Rather than being a virtue, humility in the ancient world was something despicable, indicating a cowering, cringing, subservient attitude. However, the teachings of Jesus Christ presented humility as a noble virtue. He set the example for others by humbling Himself, and of all the world's religious and ethical teachers only He put before us a little child as our model. The word that Paul uses here for humility literally means "lowliness of mind." It indicates the humble recognition of the worth, the value and the importance of other people. Paul used the same word in Philippians 2:3-8, where he described the humble mind of Christ that led Him to empty Himself and become a servant.

An old saying declares, "Coming events cast their shadows before them." When disunity walks through the church, it casts its shadow, and it's in the shape of pride. When harmony walks through, it casts its shadow before it, and it's in the fashion of humility. Pride is behind all discord—the conceit that despises other people, or the vanity that demands their respect. On the other hand, the great secret of unity is humility. Have you ever noticed how we instinctively and immediately like the people who seem to be giving us the respect we think we deserve, and instinctively dislike the people who treat us like mud? Personal vanity is a chief determinant in our relationships. There is no trap into which we so easily fall as pride, and yet there is no vice that is more frequently, more emphatically, and more eloquently condemned in Scripture. Pride is a groundless and mindless characteristic, entirely without profit and altogether destructive.

Paul exhorts each Christian to "examine his own work, and then he will have rejoicing in himself alone, and not in another" (Gal. 6:4). When we compare ourselves—our works, our gifts, our virtues—with someone else (who, of course, doesn't quite measure up), we may look terrific. But how do we stack up when we measure ourselves by the perfection of Jesus Christ? Whether ego is inflated or deflated depends on the standard with which we compare ourselves. The Christian standard is Jesus Christ, and that fact will not allow us to feed our vanity by comparing ourselves with others that we feel do not measure up to us. There is no doubt that some Christians are more gifted than others, but those talented ones should respond with humble gratitude and more fruitful service, not with haughty boasting. If divine favor has freely granted to us all the good we have, in what can we glory? A Christian's humblest hour is when he compares what he is with what he ought to be in light of

Christ's perfection, and when he compares what he has done with what he should have done in the light of Christ's commands and expectations.

The great English pastor Charles Spurgeon said that if he heard Balaam's ass using the language of man he would impute it to a miracle of God, but if he heard a Christian using the braying of vanity he would count it a miracle of another way, not of God but of Satan. The prophet speaks of the Lord's requirement that we walk **humbly** with Him (Micah 6:8), and that is the proper position for a Christian to be in when he is in fellowship with God and with other Christians.

Perhaps a word of caution is in order here lest there be a misunderstanding of just what humility is. Humility is not to depreciate yourself, not to underrate yourself. It is no humility for a person to think less of himself than he ought. Quite simply, humility is to make a right estimate of yourself. It is to see yourself as God sees you. If we have gifts and talents, humility does not deny nor silence them, but acknowledges that since God gives them, they must be used for His glory and for the edification of others. Furthermore, humility prohibits the use of those gifts for self-glory. For example, while Paul thought of himself as "not worthy to be called an apostle" (1 Cor. 15:9), he vigorously asserted and defended his apostolic calling and authority, because the truth of the gospel he preached was at stake. In other words, he used his position as an apostle to serve God and other, but never to call attention to himself. Quite unlike Paul's humble attitude is that of a man who approached me at a conference and presented himself with a self-aggrandizing introduction. His exact words were: "I'm Apostle and Prophet, Reverend Doctor Bishop . . . " While he was elevating himself, I was thinking that if he were truly deserving of any of those titles, he wouldn't have to bray about it. Can we not practice the attitude of Paul and surrender every proud pretension or conceited claim, acknowledging that we have no power of ourselves, but that it all comes from God? God does not condemn you when you accept yourself and your gifts. He just does not want us to think **more highly** of ourselves than we ought to—or **less highly** than we ought to (Rom. 12:3)

Gentleness, or as the word is often translated, **meekness**, is not weakness. We may speak of the mild-mannered Clark Kent as "meek," but remember that Moses was a meek man (Num. 12:3), yet he exercised tremendous power. Jesus Christ was "gentle and lowly in heart" (Matt. 11:29), yet He was far from weak and effeminate. The word always carries the thought of controlled power or channeled strength. For instance, secular Greek uses the word to describe a wild stallion that has been domesticated and trained to obey the word of command. Sometimes the word describes the harnessing of a strong wind. In each case there is power, but that power is under control. Applied to the character, meekness is the gentleness of the strong personality who is nevertheless the master of himself and the servant of others.

The ancient Greek philosopher Aristotle furnishes us with a vivid illustration of the meaning of gentleness when applied to our relationships with others. He defined every virtue as "the golden mean" between two extremes. On the one hand there is the extreme of excess; on the other hand there is the extreme of defect; and in between there is the happy medium. For example, at one extreme is the spendthrift; at the other extreme is the miser; and in between there is the generous person. Aristotle defined meekness as the mean between excessive anger and no anger at all. Thus, he described a meek individual as one who is always angry at the right time, and never angry at the wrong time. Put into a Christian context, then meekness or gentleness is that quality of moderation that causes us to be indignant at the wrongs done to other people, but does not allow us to harbor smoldering resentment at the injuries and insults that we have to bear.

The unity of Kingdom citizens can only be preserved when the qualities enumerated in Ephesians 4:2 are present. Every one of those virtues depends on one thing—the obliteration of self. As long as self is the hub of our relationships, as long as we insist on self-honor and self-prestige, the manifestation of our oneness is impossible. Love unites, but selfishness divides. If self predominates in the Christian society, whether speaking of individuals, local churches, or denominations, then we will be nothing more than a disintegrated collection of individualistic units. But when self is annihilated and Christ is exalted, then comes the togetherness that the world is waiting to see.

Sound Doctrine

While we should all be eager for the visible expression of Christian unity, we must never sacrifice fundamental truth in order to achieve it. There are those who call upon us to forget doctrine altogether and simply to love one another. I heard a pastor say, "I know longer preach about sin and judgment and the need to repent. I don't want to drive people away. I want them to feel loved." He is part of the so-called "Emerging Church" or "Seeker Friendly" movement that ignores biblical teaching and flows with the tide of public opinion in attracting new members. However, a spiritual enterprise built on anything other than biblical truth is standing on a very shaky foundation. Before Paul discussed spiritual unity in his letter to the Ephesians, he spent three chapters laying a doctrinal foundation. The key to the exposition of the fourth chapter of Ephesians is the word "therefore" in the first verse. That word points back to the first three chapters and emphasizes the fact that the theme of unity is something that follows as a consequence of what Paul has already written. This method is a standard practice in the New

Testament, particularly in Paul's letters. He always laid a doctrinal foundation and then he gave the application. Sound conduct is always the outcome of truth and of teaching. So in his Ephesian letter, Paul does not start with unity and then proceed to doctrine; he discusses unity because he has already presented his doctrine.

Therefore, if the doctrine expounded in the first three chapters is the basis and the background for everything Paul has to say about unity, it is essential that we understand that doctrine. In general, the great theme of the first half of Ephesians is redemption through the shedding of the blood of Christ on the cross. Paul reminds his readers that they are people who have realized that all their own good works, all their own righteousness, their nationality, and everything they might contribute, are entirely useless in achieving salvation. They became Christians and came into this unity that is in the church entirely by the action of the Lord Jesus Christ. "But now in Christ Jesus you who were once far off have been brought near by the blood of Christ" (Eph. 2:13). No one can ever belong to the family of God, and participate in its unity, who has never come personally to know God the Father through the reconciling work of Jesus Christ and by the power of the Holy Spirit.

Elsewhere Paul expresses his concern that Christians not break the unity of the Spirit by agreeing with false doctrine (Rom. 16:17-20), and John echoes this warning (2 John 6-11). The church must never believe in peace at any price, for God's wisdom is "first pure, then peaceable" (James 3:17). Unity, then, is not something that exists in and of itself. It is the inevitable result of our belief and acceptance of this great and glorious doctrine of God who has provided in Christ the way of salvation, and unity must never be thought of except in terms of that doctrine. While all genuine Christians do not agree on minor matters, they all do agree on the foundational truths of the faith. Therefore, I do not ask what denominational label you wear, or whether you call your pastor "Father" or "Reverend" or

"Brother," whether you were sprinkled or immersed. I simply ask if you have been redeemed by the blood of Jesus, born of the Spirit, and if Christ reigns as Lord in your life. Here is the basis of unity.

Unfortunately, doctrinal purity of itself does not guarantee the outward manifestation of spiritual unity, because there are individuals and churches that are sound in faith, but unsound when it comes to love. This is why Paul joins the two: "speaking the truth in love" (Eph. 4:15).

The Lordship of Jesus Christ

The German philosopher Schopenhauer compared people to a pack of porcupines on a freezing winter night. The extreme cold forces them together for warmth. But as soon as they press very close, they jab and hurt one another. So they separate again, only vainly to attempt over and over again to huddle together. This sad, semi-humorous picture of humanity teaches us that something must be yielded if we are to live in unity. The citizens of the Kingdom of God ought to regard, love and treat one another as brothers and sisters. However, it is a strange and unhappy fact that many individual Christians, local churches and denominations are distinguished less by loving acceptance than by critical rejection. That situation is not entirely new, for Paul dealt with it in the first century. So we can learn valuable lessons for contemporary church life from his instructions to the early Christians.

The chief lesson of Romans 14 is that when we acknowledge Jesus as Lord our relationship to one another is right. The chapter deals with the "weaker brother," the Christian with a weak, under-developed and over-sensitive conscience. One of the issues involved was whether Christians could eat meat. Those with strong conscience saw nothing wrong with eating meat, but those with a weak one became vegetarians. Another issue involved the observance of days.

Some people regarded certain days as better and more important than others, while others regarded all days as alike. So the Christians in the church at Rome had differences of opinion about certain foods and days.

There is nothing wrong in differences of opinion about minor matters. Naturally, as we have seen, we must be in agreement about the major doctrines and all the fundamentals of the faith. But we are only being realistic when we admit that we are not going to agree with one another totally until we get to heaven. Meanwhile, Christians have got to learn to be tolerant of one another in the Christian family. Don't we learn to tolerate one another's idiosyncrasies in the human family? A famous epigram, attributed to a certain Rupert Meldenius, eloquently teaches the point I am making:

In essentials unity,

In non-essentials liberty,

In all things charity.

The thing that concerned Paul was not the existence of minor differences, but the attitudes the Christians had toward one another because of their differences. They despised one another and sat in judgment on one another (Rom. 14:2-3). In Romans 14 Paul dealt with the situation theologically. He didn't stop with just an appeal to those Roman Christians to be nice and kind and tolerant. Instead, he reminded them of a doctrine that they had forgotten or weren't applying to their situation. It concerned the lordship of Jesus Christ. He had died and risen again "that He might be Lord" (v. 9), and that in consequence "if we live, we live to the Lord" (v. 8), for after death we will have to give an account of ourselves to Him (vs. 10-12). Therefore, every Christian, in life and death, is the servant of Jesus Christ. Since this is true, "who are you to judge the servant of another?" (v. 4). It is no business of ours to despise or judge any servant of Jesus Christ, because “to his own master he stands or falls (v. 4).

The lesson Paul is teaching becomes clearer when you understand that he thought the weaker brethren were wrong. He himself was not a vegetarian and he didn’t see any reason why he shouldn’t eat meat that had been offered in sacrifice to idols. He knew that idols were nothing; they didn’t exist. He could eat such meat with thanksgiving without any scruples at all. But, he explains in verses 13-23 and in 1 Corinthians 8, a “strong” Christian must voluntarily curb his own liberty of conscience in the presence of a weak brother or sister lest he cause them to do something against their conscience. In other words, Christian love limits Christian liberty. Scripture has a very high view of the human conscience, and even when a conscience is weak and uneducated, it must still be respected.

The secret, then, of our relations with one another in the Christian church, especially when we have differences, is the recognition that Jesus Christ is Lord and that we live unto Him. To despise or stand in judgment on a fellow Christian on trivial matters is not just a breach of fellowship. It is actually a denial of the Lordship of Jesus Christ. It is a presumptuous attempt to usurp His prerogative as Lord. Who am I that I should assume the role of another Christian’s lord and judge? Jesus is the Lord and judge of the whole church, and I have no right to interfere with the administration of His rule. It is before Him that we stand or fall. If we acknowledge Jesus as Lord, then immediately our relations with one another in the fellowship of the church are put right.

The Nature of Unity

If we are to preserve the unity that we already have, it will help to understand the nature of that unity. The New Testament discusses the unity of Christians in both physical and spiritual terms.

The apostle Paul particularly favored the **physical analogy**, in which the church is described as the body of Christ. He worked it out most extensively in Romans 12 and 1 Corinthians 12, where in both places he taught that the spiritual gifts possessed by individuals are to be used for the benefit of the whole. Ephesians 4:16 gives a concise summary of the lesson: "From whom the whole body, joined and knit together by what every joint supplies, according to the effective working by which every part does its share, causes growth of the body for the edifying of itself in love."

The various passages containing the body metaphor suggest at least three ideas concerning the church:

Unity. The body is one (1 Cor. 12:13-20; Eph. 4:4). The marvel of the human body is that, while it consists of many different parts having various functions, they are all one, bound together in a vital manner. It is not a matter of fingers being stuck on to hands, and hands to wrists, and so on. It is all one. All the parts come out of an original cell, and they are all extensions and manifestations of that original germ of life. The unity in the church is like that.

Diversity. The one body has many members (Rom. 12:4; 1 Cor. 12:14). Even as the human body consists of many members with different functions, so the church consists of members with various gifts (Rom. 12:5ff; 1 Cor. 12; Eph. 4:7-16). In each case there is unity in diversity. Indeed, diversity is of the very essence of the body, but there is unity in that all members are essential one to the other.

Responsibility. Just as the limbs and organs of the body have mutual need of one another, there are duties of ministry one to another within the body of Christ (1Cor. 12:15-31). The Holy Spirit imparts various gifts to various individuals, and we are responsible to use those gifts to serve God and other Christians in such a way that Christ is glorified and believers are edified. If every member recognized his

God-assigned responsibility, many would be saved from inferiority, envy, or pride, and the growth of the fellowship would be fostered.

The **spiritual reality** of the unity of Christians is seen by the fact that it is comparable to the unity that exists between the Father and the Son. The prayer of Jesus in John 17:20-23 clearly teaches this comparison:

> I do not pray for these alone, but also for those who will believe in Me through their word; that they all may be one, as You, Father, are in Me and I in You; that they also may be one in Us, that the world may believe that You sent Me. And the glory which You gave Me I have given them, that they may be one just as We are one: I in them, and You in Me; that they may be made perfect in one."

It should be obvious from these verses that Jesus is not speaking of some external organizational unity. When He speaks of the mystical union that subsists between the three persons of the Trinity, He is speaking of a unity of essence. Here is the mystery of the Trinity. There are three persons and yet but one God. And what makes them one is not simply a unity of interest and thought and purpose and love, but the unity of essence and substance. Therefore, the unity of Christians is something that involves this unity of essence. According to Peter, Christians are "partakers of the divine nature" (2 Pet. 1:4), and our unity is by virtue of the fact that we all have received that new nature through a new birth. Apart from the work of the Holy Spirit who creates within believers this new nature, there can be no unity at all as Jesus spoke of it.

In other words, the unity that Jesus is talking about in John 17 is a unity that can only be obtained among those who are born again and thus are "partakers of the divine nature." It is more than a matter of friendship, and more than a group of people forming a coalition to carry out certain purposes. It is a family relationship. When a person is born physically, he is born into a family, and though he may disagree with members of that family, there is still a relationship of blood and essence. So is the unity of the church. Our unity is the result of being born into a family, sharing the same nature. What Jesus taught in John 14:23 is true of every individual Christian: "If anyone loves Me, he will keep My word, and My Father will love him, and We will come to him and make Our home with him."

Let us then, by the charitableness of our conduct and the soundness of our doctrine, by mutual submission to the lordship of Jesus Christ, and by recognition of the fact that we are one in essence, endeavor "to keep the unity of the Spirit." If we do that, we will not constantly waste time seeking for structures of unity, nor press for a dead, dull, monotonous uniformity of church life and liturgy. On the contrary, we will be a humble, loving community rejoicing in the diversity of ministries that God has designed to enrich and enliven the membership of the body of Christ. As such our fellowship will ever be deepening and will be marked by a steady growth into maturity by holding the truth in love, and we shall understand the truth of Psalm 133:1: "Behold, how good and how pleasant it is for brethren to dwell together in unity!"

VII

KINGDOM WITNESS

The Kingdom of God is a family affair, in which citizens enjoy fellowship with their Father, who is the King, and with each other. However, we must not seek fellowship as an end in itself, nor allow the Christian community to degenerate into an introspective club. Fellowship that exists for nothing but its own satisfaction will wither, and a church whose members are only a self-regarding coterie of smug and selfish recluses, interested only in themselves, has forfeited its right to be called a church at all. The Christian church is the only society in the world that exists for the benefit of those who are not members, because it always reaches beyond itself to those still outside its fellowship. However, there is a real danger that we can become so absorbed in our own interior life that we abandon the outside world.

What can we say of those Christians who have the attitude that they should be recipients instead of givers? Too many of our number think that they are to attend services, sit in the pews and receive teaching. Then by paying a salary to "full-time" Christian workers they can hire the spreading of the faith. Such a notion is completely foreign to New Testament Christianity. The church has got to leave its own secure borders and move out into the world. If there is no such outward movement, then the fellowship stagnates, the Spirit is quenched and withdraws Himself, and the deposit of religiosity that is left becomes putrefaction in the lives of those who have grieved Him.

Not long ago a certain church planned an evangelistic campaign to reach the unsaved people in the community. The members set a date, booked an evangelist and printed advertising, and then suddenly, they came to a terrible realization. None of them had any unsaved friends. They had lived to themselves, drifting into a Christian fellowship that had alienated them from the world. As a result, they had become inbred to the point that they were absolutely sterile.

A false idea of separation lies behind this situation. Withdrawal was the attitude of the Pharisees, whose very name means "separatists." But Jesus does not want His followers to be Christian Pharisees. Yet, a pharisaic attitude among Christians is more common than we are willing to admit. Too many times as we enjoy the security of our praise gatherings and teaching seminars, we present to the outsider an image of the church that is often not inviting but forbidding, smugly satisfied with itself and harshly condemning of others. Is it without reason that some non-Christians say that they find more acceptance and more compassionate understanding in the worldly kingdom than in the Kingdom of God? Let us by all means keep our fellowship from deteriorating into an introverted clique lest the church become a preserve for the impeccably respectable, a museum of rare spiritual exhibits where the sin-sick cannot find convalescence nor the helpless find refuge. We are not to be a private club comprised of spiritual spectators. We can easily isolate ourselves, remaining way over here going through the motions of religion, while the people who need us are way over there. Some of our churches have become citadels where once or twice a week the army marches around inside the fortress and has bayonet practice and so forth, but they never make contact with the enemy on the battlefield. That's the same as keeping salt in the shaker and never applying it where it's needed.

Closely akin to the pharisaic self-righteousness that causes many Christians to isolate themselves is a fear of contamination from the world, which, however genuine it may be, leads to a spirit of monasticism. It was this concern that prompted the hermits to flee into the desert in the fourth century A.D. and led to the development of monasticism in the Middle Ages. And that same attitude is still present in the church. Some of our fellowships are in reality evangelical monasteries, although without stone walls and without the name. Perhaps this hope to withdraw from the world's pollution is understandable, because it begins with a desire to obey the commands not to love the world (1 John 2:15-17), nor to be conformed to it (Rom. 12:2), but rather to keep oneself unstained from the world (James 1:27). However, while the intent is commendable, the logic is deplorable, because it assumes that the only effective way to avoid conformity to worldly standards is to avoid the company of worldly people, and the way to renounce worldliness is to out of the world. Monasticism, whatever form it may take, is not truly Christian ideal. This assertion is plain from the petition of Jesus in John 17:15: "I do not pray that You should take them out of the world, but that You should keep them from the evil one."

I call for all Christian groups to conduct a sincere self-examination to determine if a monastic outlook is present. Are you living a life of religious seclusion, insulated from the world? Do you show little or no concern for others outside your own fellowship, being pre-occupied rather with the business of self-preservation? The church of the New Testament was not a secret society, existing for its own private benefits. On the contrary, the first believers recognized themselves as the body of Christ, existing for Christ's purposes in the world. They never sang, as their present-day successors sometimes sing:

We are a garden wall'd around,

Chosen and made peculiar ground:

A little spot enclos'd by grace

Out of the world's wide wilderness.

--Isaac Watts

That kind of attitude can easily lead to an ecclesiastical self-absorption in which the members of the fellowship have no concern to live in the world as both witnesses and servants. Fellowship that exists as an end in itself will not survive, simply because it is not Christian. The purpose of the fellowship is to be out in the world living Christ, scattering the glory and heralding the Lord. And it is the very death of the fellowship if it fails its Master in this regard.

Jesus is our example in relating to the world. He did not remain aloof, hiding away in the safe immunity of heaven. He actually entered our world, assuming our nature, identifying Himself with our humanity, exposing Himself to our temptations, befriending outcasts and earning the reputation of being "a friend of tax collectors and sinners" (Luke 7:34). Now He says to the church, "As the Father has sent Me, I also send you" (John 20:21; see 17:18). So Christ sends us into the world on a mission like that of His own, not to run away and escape, not to stand aloof from the world, but to enter it, to penetrate it, for His glory. Nothing but costly involvement is Christian, and any kind of withdrawal is pharisaic. The early church thrived among people whom the religious hierarchy shunned. How would you like to be a member of a church where most of the congregation consists of former fornicators, idolaters, adulterers, perverts, homosexuals, thieves, drunkards, revilers and swindlers? Such people as that were part of a New Testament fellowship (1 Cor. 6:9-11). Are we going to display the grudging, judging attitude of the elder brother, the false pharisaic fear of contamination-by-contact, or the compassionate identification of Christ, of whom it was charged: "This man receives sinners and eats with them" (Luke 15:2)?

It is not enough for us to enjoy the goodies of our internal fellowship and expect outsiders to come to the feast. Christ expects His witnesses to take the initiative. "You shall receive power when the Holy Spirit has come upon you; and you shall be witnesses to Me," He said (Acts 1:8). This proclamation is the Lord's standing order to all His followers, and we can no more restrict the command to witness than we can restrict the promise of the Spirit.

Jesus graphically described Christians as "the salt of the earth" and "the light of the world" (Matt. 5:13-14). Those metaphors indicate that there is an essential difference between two communities—the church and the world. On the one hand there is the "earth"; on the other hand there is "the salt of the earth." On the one hand there is the "world"; on the other hand there is "the light of the world." The analogies of Jesus tell us that the world is a dark place, with little or no light of its own, and it manifests a constant tendency to deteriorate or putrefy. The world cannot stop itself from going bad. Followers of Christ, on the other hand, are set in the world with a double role to fulfill. As salt they are to arrest, or at least to hinder, the process of social decay; and as light they are to illumine the darkness. If we are put here as salt, the world must be decaying; if we are put here as light, the world must be full of darkness. When God saved us, He saved us to live in a world that needs us. Who else is "blameless and harmless, children of God without fault in the midst of a crooked and perverse generation, among whom you shine as lights in the world" (Phil. 2:15)? And who else is "a light that shines in a dark place" (2 Pet. 1:19)?

The first chapter of Romans presents a grim picture of what happens when society rejects what it knows and extinguishes whatever light it has by nature. Society deteriorates, its values and standards steadily decline until it becomes utterly corrupt, and God gives evildoers over to their own lusts and passions, until society stinks in the nostrils both of God and of all decent men and women. God sets citizens of His Kingdom into the midst of that stinking secular society, not to recoil and withdraw into little monastic ghettos and establishments, but to penetrate that rotten darkness for Christ. We must never allow the church to become a cold-storage chamber where we stock and hide away our personal faith and witness. Rather, we are to let it be a powerhouse, sending out into the world the light and warmth and radiance of the Christ.

At this point a word of caution is necessary. Some well-intended Christians, in their desire to identify with unbelievers and tear down barriers, have become assimilated to the outlook and standards of the world, thus erasing the distinction between the church and the world. There is a strange teaching today that says it makes no difference where you go and what you do; just become a part of what you're trying to reach. Such an attitude is far from that of Jesus. It is true that He was "a friend of tax collectors and sinners" (Luke 7:34), but it is also true that He was "holy, harmless, undefiled, separate from sinners" (Heb. 7:26). There is a danger that by coming in contact with this decaying world we start to lose our flavor. De-salted salt is useless, and so also is a de-Christianized Christian. For effectiveness in the community the Christian has got to retain his Christ-likeness; otherwise his influence is lost. Remember that Jesus said we are the **salt** of the earth, not the **sugar**. Salt retards corruption, but sugar only hastens it. Therefore, like our King, we should be both "worldly" (involved in the life of the world) and "holy" (distinct from the standards of the world) simultaneously. In other words, we are to maintain a "holy worldliness," being in the world while not of it, like the beautiful lily I once saw growing on a dung heap in a barnyard. If you put a boat in the water, the boat floats; but if you put the water in the boat, the boat sinks. Put the church in the world, and the church, while in the world, floats above its pollution; put the world in the church, and the church sinks.

While individual members of the fellowship are to engage in active witnessing, there is also to be a forceful witness exuding from the corporate fellowship. The very fact that people with different personalities, of different races and national origins, from different backgrounds and social strata, can live together in the loving harmony described in the New Testament is in itself an almost irresistible attraction. It was that kind of witness that enabled the first Christian community in Jerusalem to have "favor with all the people" (Acts 2:47). Kosher barriers soon broke down among the first believers, because they found it ridiculous to tolerate any man-made barriers since they were united as brothers and sisters in Christ. That kind of fellowship was revolutionary in the ancient world, and it still is today. It raises the eyebrows when such improbable partners as senators and prisoners sit down together in Christian fellowship at Fellowship House in Washington. But unless our churches demonstrate to outsiders a quality of love and caring that surpasses anything in the world, we will not be demonstrating the power of the gospel; we will only be talking about it. And speech without demonstration will not convince anybody for long.

This attraction, of course, begins with individual Christian lives. Jesus Himself attracted sinners of the worst kind. "All the tax collectors and the sinners drew near to Him to hear Him" (Luke 15:1). What the Pharisees meant as an insult when they called Him a friend of crooks and other sinners was actually the greatest compliment they could give Him. Many years ago Satan began to circulate the false idea that the more we become like Jesus the farther away unsaved people want to stay from us. The opposite is true. Sinners saw something in Jesus that they needed and wanted, and it's the same today with those who follow after Christ.

However, as I have indicated, people are drawn to Christ not only by the example of individual Christians, but also by the corporate life of the entire Christian community. The pastor of a large church submitted a questionnaire to the membership in which he asked what first attracted them to Christ. Three-fourths responded that their first attraction was something they had seen in Christian people, either as individuals or as a group. For example, one person was "immensely attracted by the Christian love and friendship of the believers in the church fellowship to which I belonged." Another described "a gradual awareness that there was 'life' in the fellowship which I knew nothing of."

Of even greater interest is an article written by a veteran missionary to India. He had questioned a number of leading Indian Christians concerning their attraction to the Christian faith. It was not the longing for personal salvation. In almost every case it was Christian love and concern. Some responded that it was the freedom of the Christian family that impressed them—the attraction of the fellowship in Christ as compared to the bondage of caste. Others were drawn to the gospel by the thought of Christ uniting into one the divided races and peoples of India. They saw in the Christian community a truly inter-racial, inter-social fellowship, whose members evidently cared for one another and bore one another's burdens, and tat to them was a forceful witness to the reconciling power of Jesus Christ.

There can be no doubt that this is the witness that Jesus was talking about when He said, "By this all will know that you are My disciples, if you have love for one another" (John 13:35), and when He prayed, "That they all may be one, as You, Father, are in Me, and I in You, that they also may be one in Us, that the world may believe that You sent Me" (John 17:21). It is by their love for one another that the world recognizes Christ's disciples, and it is by the witness of their fellowship that the world comes to belief in Christ.

In the first Christian communities, peasants sat together with trained professionals; slaves with those of high society; Gentiles with Jews; the poor with the rich; and the unlearned with the educated. Everybody referred to one another as "Brother," and they really meant it, because they "were of one heart and one soul" (Acts 4:32). They customarily met together for fraternal meals and "breaking bread from house to house" (Acts 2:46). By the unwavering strength of their faith and their joyful endurance under persecution, but most of all by the obvious love they had for each other, they were true witnesses of Christ whom they professed.

The strength of the fellowship as a witness to the world becomes even more evident when John 1:18 and 1 John 4:12 are brought together. Both verses begin with the words, "No one has seen God at any time." That is precisely the problem with people the world over, whose philosophy is "seeing is believing." How can they believe in a God who is invisible to them? The first answer is that God has made Himself visible in Jesus Christ: "No one has ever seen God; but God's only Son . . . has made him known" (John 1:18 NEB). As a result of the incarnation Jesus could declare, "He who has seen Me has seen the Father" (John 14:9). However, unbelievers may argue that Jesus is not on the earth today, and God is still invisible. He may have appeared once on earth as "the image of the invisible God" (Col. 1:15), but that was two thousand years ago. How then can God be seen today? Listen to the surprising answer in 1 John 4:12: "No one has seen God at any time. If we love one another, God abides in us, and His love has been perfected in us." John is actually saying that the invisible God who revealed Himself in His Son now reveals Himself in His people, in the love that they have for one another, which is really the love of God. In His prayer to the Father, Jesus stated it like this: "I have glorified You on the earth . . . and I am glorified in them" (John 17:4, 10). Christ, who glorified and manifested the Father on earth, is Himself glorified and manifested in Christians. If, then, we are to witness effectively to the world, all of God's people must exhibit the contagious fellowship presented to us in the New Testament.

Again, we look to the early church for an example. Acts 5:12-18; 40-42 gives a vivid account of the power resulting from the fellowship of the first Christian community. First, that Christian fellowship had **power to repel**. "They used to meet by common consent in Solomon's Portico, not one from outside their number venturing to join with them" (vs. 12-13 NEB). The fact that outsiders were somewhat in awe of the people of God is reminiscent of Deuteronomy 23:10, which declares: "Then all peoples of the earth shall see that you are called by the name of the Lord, and they shall be afraid of you." The joyful fellowship of Christians not only emits light that beckons earnest searchers; it flames with a fire that frightens pretenders. Today many pastors are so numbers conscious that they can't see the difference between a Gideon's three hundred and a mob. Will we ever learn that bulk can never be a substitute for power, and that obesity is not the same as growth? Some of the biggest bodies are the sickest. The fellowship described in the New Testament, which is demanding in its commitment, will always scare away Satan's quislings and the world's Judases. It burns with a holy flame that will scorch the hypocritical fraternizer and will make the compromiser sweat. Let's never be guilty of doting on statistics to the extent that we forsake separation for compromise. Success is not in numbers. The real solution is in an exodus—a turning out of those who should never have been taken in. Thousands of people have been amiably cajoled into church membership without the vital prerequisite of a new birth. Perhaps this situation has resulted from pushing a human program rather than pleading the divine presence. At any rate, true Christian fellowship will repel the false in order to safeguard and demonstrate the real.

The fellowship of the first Christians also had **power to attract**, and when we look at our highly structured institutions of today, it's amazing to us how they did it. That early church did not coerce; they did not resort to trickery; they did not rely on publicity stunts. It didn't boast of academic scholarship or millionaire members, and it had no streamlined administration. Yet it had an attraction that dumbfounded the hostile bigots at the head of the *status quo*. The fifth chapter of Acts reveals that the church attracted two classes of people. First, it attracted believers, who came for fellowship: "And believers were increasingly added to the Lord, multitudes of both men and women" (v. 14). Every true Christian reaches out for fellowship with other members of the household of faith. We have seen that believers are a family sharing a common experience. They long for fellowship with one another because that same Spirit of life in each of them yearns toward all other members of the family.

Unfortunately, the contemporary church often does not approximate the magnetic fellowship of the first church because there is among us a spiritual superficiality and a commitment that demands very little of us. Many modern-day Christians are nothing more than ecclesiastical gypsies, wandering from one church to another, never allowing themselves to become involved in the "one-anotherness" that New Testament fellowship requires.

A second group of people that the first church attracted was the sick, who came for healing:

> They brought the sick out into the streets and laid them on beds and couches, that at least the shadow of Peter passing by might fall on some of them. Also a multitude gathered from the surrounding cities to Jerusalem, bringing sick people and those who were tormented by unclean spirits, and they were all healed (vs. 15-16).

Healing for the body is included in the Spirit's gifts to the church. That healing includes not only physical illnesses, but all other kinds of illness as well. A lot of people need saving almost as much from the pharmacist as from the devil. There are no tranquilizers sold over the druggist's counter that can compare with the healing tranquility administered by the Holy Spirit in the midst of a loving, caring, praying fellowship. Mark 2:1 states that news circulated in Capernaum that Jesus was in the house, while Luke 5:17 says that the power of the Lord was present to heal. If our churches were living and operating in the fullness of the Holy Spirit, news would continuously circulate that Jesus is in the house and that the power of the Lord is present to heal. Such churches are as magnetic now as the church of two thousand years ago was magnetic then.

The first church had the power to repel and the power to attract, and it also had the **power to overcome**. Acts 5:17 describes trouble threatening the church. The jealous and envious religious leaders imprisoned the apostles and later flogged them and ordered them to cease preaching Jesus. But notice how the chapter ends:

> So they departed from the presence of the council, rejoicing that they were counted worthy to suffer shame for His name. And daily in the temple, and in every house, they did not cease teaching and preaching Jesus as the Christ (vs. 41, 42).

Their dynamic fellowship survived every crisis and was victorious in every situation. For them new difficulty only meant new opportunity, and new trial only meant new triumph. The enemy can never destroy a church like that, with its members committed to one another in the strength of fellowship and empowered by the Holy Spirit.

We simply must get back to the New Testament pattern. If you want spiritual power in your church, start paying attention to the quality of the fellowship. Too seldom is a church able to echo

Jacob's words at Bethel: "Surely the Lord is in this place . . . How awesome is this place! This is none other than the house of God, and this is the gate of heaven!" (Gen. 18:16, 17). New Testament fellowship does not stop with itself; it causes us to look away from ourselves to the world outside our circle, and to vow to one another the loyalty that it will take to storm and conquer the world for Christ. The perfect unity between the Father and the Son is to be manifested in the personal relationships of believers, so that the world, seeing that unity in love, might believe. We will convince the unbelieving world by the very quality of our own fellowship, and outsiders will recognize that we are disciples of Christ, and that He is sent from God. Let us all cooperate to fulfill our Lord's prayer in John 17:20-23, and by the quality of our mutual love, fellowship and unity, compel unbelievers in our own age to exclaim, not in sarcasm but in wonder, "See how these Christians love one another!"

CONCLUSION

There remains much to be said about relationships among Kingdom citizens. For instance, I have given no practical suggestions concerning the mechanics of promoting fellowship, such as establishing cell groups in which participants may freely share with one another their trials and triumphs and may both give and receive support as part of a company that really cares. However, those suggestions lie outside the scope of this study, and far more qualified teachers than I have dealt adequately with them in their writings. Therefore, I defer to their experience and wisdom.

I exhort every Christian not to think of the church as a mere international organization, but rather to understand it as a supra-national organism. And I emphasize again the need each individual Christian has for this family of God that transcends all natural barriers tending to separate us. You need the rest of the family, and they need you. Make certain that in your relationships at large you make time to develop a close fellowship with others who love your King, for the Christian life is not a solitary existence; it is a family affair. I am more and more convinced that the Christian life involves more than just a private, mystical relationship with Christ, to be enjoyed in the isolation of a vacuum. Christian character has no significance apart from Christian relationships. Fellowship in the family is vital if you are going to make a success of the Christian life. Someone wisely observed that Christianity that does not begin with the individual does not begin, but Christianity that ends with the individual ends.

I warn you that the fellowship presented to us in the New Testament is demanding, tough and costly. You will find it easier to be a Sunday morning Christian, showing your respect for the Lord by occupying your spot in the pew and paying your dies when the offering plate is passed. But a gospel that does not demand my submission to other members of the body of Christ is not the gospel of the New Testament, and it will never bear witness to a hostile, sarcastic world that challenges us to demonstrate in some tangible manner what we piously profess to believe.

Many before you have shrunk away from the demands of living in the kind of Kingdom relationships that the King expects of His subjects. Perhaps they do so for other reasons than reluctance to get involved with the lives of other people. Perhaps they fear unmasking themselves and having their faults known to others. Or perhaps it's the fear of exploitation or of disappointment or failure. Or could it be a false sense of independence that reflects the supposedly heroic attitude (stoic but not Christian) that sets its chin and declares, "I can go it alone without anybody's help"? If you are among that number, not letting anyone know what your struggles are, but in self-sufficiency trying to be self-convincing that you need no human fellowship to help you, then you are guilty of a pride of the grossest kind. You will never find God's way for you by clinging to that attitude of stubborn independence.

Others who shrink from the demands of costly New Testament Kingdom relationships withdraw into a more superficial and comfortable group, either one where they can be in control, or one that offers no real challenge. Those who opt for that kind of fellowship will find themselves drifting along in the mediocrity and conformity that characterizes so much of modern society and the Christian church, just "one of the group." That kind of childish dependence will never lead toward spiritual maturity.

But neither mulish **independence** nor debilitating **dependence** is the King's plan for His subjects. We will "all come to the unity of the faith and of the knowledge of the Son of God, to a perfect man, to the measure of the stature of the fullness of

Christ" (Eph. 4:13) only in the healthy **interdependence** of the body of Christ, through a fellowship where love is actively worked out in "one-anotherness."

Christian fellowship now is the earthly counterpart and foretaste of the eternal fellowship of heaven. Fellowship here is the earthly model of eternal communion with God and with fellow believers, and it shares the same spiritual nature as life in heaven. If we don't get along here, what isolated ghettos will we be able to find in heaven? And if you don't love me here, will you be able to avoid me in heaven?

Printed in Dunstable, United Kingdom

63775875R00087